IN THE MOOD FOR PEACE:
THE STORY OF THE IZZY DOLL
by
Phyllis Wheaton

Copyright © 2011 Phyllis Wheaton

First Printing January 2012, Blitzprint Inc., Calgary, Alberta, Canada
Second Printing September 2012, Apache Superior Printing Ltd. Calgary, Alberta, Canada

Library and Archives Canada Cataloguing in Publication

Project Co-ordinator / Research / Author: Phyllis Wheaton, Calgary, Alberta, Canada, www.phylliswheaton.com

Project Editor : Pat Kozak, Calgary, Alberta, Canada

Cover/Content Design : Jason Clough, Blue Rain Creative, Calgary, Alberta, Canada, www.blueraincreative.com

Wheaton, Phyllis 1955-   In the Mood for Peace : The Story of the Izzy Doll / Phyllis Wheaton.

ISBN 978-0-9681294-1-8   1. War relief. 2. Peacekeeping forces, Canadian.

3. Isfeld, Mark, 1962-1994. 4. Isfeld family. 5. Izzy doll. I. Title.

HV639.W44 2011   363.34'988   C2011-907765-5

THANK-YOU...

My heartfelt appreciation for the expert technical support and for going the extra mile, by Editor Pat Kozak and Graphic Designer Jason Clough from Blue Rain Creative.

Thank you to the Isfeld family, Judy and Leigh, Glenn, Judy MacGibbon, Pat MacKenzie, Dave and Lynn Breese and Kelly for your stories, photos and your willingness to travel through an emotional exercise of reminiscing the past.

Thank you to all those who allowed me to interview them for the book; Billy and Lynne Willbond, Shirley O'Connell and angels Lew, Don, Mollie, Mike and Paul. Thank-you Padre Paul Alain Monpas, Jim and Sharon Davis, Sophie Richard, Ben and Margie Walsh, Maureen Eykelenboom, Lloyd and Teanna Hodgins, Ed Fitch, and those I may have forgotten for the contributors were many.

Special thanks to a tremendous group of people who contributed their time and/or research and for their encouragement during the two and a half years that it took to write and publish this book. Please know that the forward movement of each chapter was propelled by your positive and critical comments, smiles, patience and support, arriving at the right time. Ellen Kelly, Marilyn Rose Brown, Audrey Kochalyk, Linda Boston, Monika Goodwin, Carol Bryson, Roberta Travis, Diana Slater, Bernice Toon, Suzie Toth, Joyce Mann, Judy McIntosh, Sandie Riemersma, Ken Holmes, Barbara Johnson, Rory M. Cory, Daryl Janz, David Bull, Bill Village, Mark Sheppard, Darryl Preece and his cousin Samantha Nickerson, Marianne and Rolland MacKenzie, Doug Sheppard, Kareen and John Jackson, Ken and Linda Johnson, Lieutenant Trevor Reid, Tom Poole, David O'Toole, Captain Derrick Forsythe, Carolyn Foard, Cpl Kyle Scott, Cpl Scott Oakley, Dan Singleton, Michael Harc of Owl's Nest Books in Calgary, Robin Legere for your Facebook page - Canadian Combat Engineers: Remembering the Fallen. Thank you Andy Holota, Rick Wright, W. Brett Wilson, Syd Burrows, John Duncan, Scott Fairweather with the Canadian Landmine Foundation, Guy Willowby with HALO Trust, Jan Randal, Stephane Grenier

And last but always first, my family for your constant support of the work I feel called to write and sing about.

TABLE OF CONTENTS

INTRODUCTION

Most often it's the little boys, shaking their arms wildly for attention to ask their questions about WWI weapons, bombs or battlefields during an education session at the Military Museum. But one day a little girl with long hair, in school uniform, sitting in the second row, raised her hand and with forthright innocence asked, "How does war end?"

How does war end?

Her question caught me and I wondered why I'd never heard it asked before. Shouldn't it actually be the question asked most often? Whatever political criteria are needed to bring an end to war, it seems obvious that the process would begin by being in the mood for peace.

Mark Isfeld, a Canadian Peacekeeper, understood that war-ending mindset and was intensely serious about saving lives in his job as a Sapper. While de-mining and bringing normalcy back to the people he was deployed to serve, Mark used the phrase, "He is truly in the mood for peace," when describing a Croatian soldier who had become his ally in detecting and destroying landmines.

Meeting Mark's parents, Carol and Brian, gave me insights into how the life of one family affected so many worldwide, both through their work with the Izzy Doll and by their participation in the movement to abolish landmines. Carol, who had crocheted dolls for her son to gift to the children he met during his deployment, admitted that she was just an ordinary woman, but her empathy for others and her tenacity to help showed how extraordinary she was. Knitters and crafters who heard about her homemade Izzy Dolls, most often mothers, grandmothers and great-grandmothers, were excited at the possibility of doing something to help. Many of these knitters were elderly Canadians who grew up during wartime and who remembered vividly the horrendous stories of war from their parents or relatives. Many felt that the making of these dolls was their contribution toward peace in the world. As of July 2011 they had knitted or crocheted an impressive one million dolls for the children of war and the poorest of the poor.

Just after their son was killed in 1994, Brian set up a memorial web site with links to Mark's letters, the Izzy Doll pattern, Peacekeeper sites, and much more. He had wanted his son's story, and the Izzy Doll legacy project, to be imbedded into our generation, imprinting who we are as Canadians. Carol's death in 2007 and Brian's passing five months later shook us all. Created in a country that values peace, made with love, and given in the spirit of friendship, the humble Izzy Doll has become a symbol of peacekeeping. In the Mood for Peace: The Story of the Izzy Doll is a testament to how our lives intrinsically connect, how one action causes a reaction, and how if we are "in the mood for peace" it can happen with the deepest intent, through the gentlest of wills. This is a compilation of the Isfeld stories and how a ball of yarn personified changed lives.

The book also includes stories about other heroes like Peacekeeper veteran Billy Willbond and his wife, Lynne, who witnessed the aftermath of war and the resulting poverty and recognized the immeasurable value of the Izzy doll to soothe and comfort a child. Relief workers, military and spiritual leaders, media, and politicians were all moved to be a part of the Izzy Doll phenomenon that extended from a basket of yarn in a Canadian living room to the arms of a needy child half way around the globe. All were in the mood for peace.

These stories are also a faith-quest, with accounts of signs and spiritual interventions that could only be called divine, that beckoned Brian and Carol to trust and believe in something greater than the tangible. And in the bigger picture it's a message for us all.

PROLOGUE

This book was almost finished when I realized that the responsibility I felt to acknowledge the families of our fallen began years before I met the Isfelds or ever heard of the Izzy Doll. It began with a visit to Signal Hill in 2001. There are four gigantic numbers on the side of this hill in southwest Calgary. 137, 113, 51, and 151. They are striking, and for me they were unforgettable. The first time I saw them

I asked everyone I met what they were, but no one seemed to know. And those who suggested answers such as "landing markers for planes" or "hockey" or "real estate" numbers were obviously guessing.

Why didn't the average citizen know the local history — especially when it was as big as life like the numbers on Signal Hill and in our face every day? I had to wonder whether Canadians were guilty of not knowing their history, or guilty of not wanting to know.

Researching the numbers took me to the Museum of the Regiments (now The Military Museums or TMM) where I discovered that they were WWI battalion numbers set in place between 1915 and 1917 by soldiers stationed at Sarcee camp near the base of the hill. Each number represented a battalion; 113 Lethbridge, 51 Edmonton, 151 Red Deer and 137 Calgary. As a result I wrote a song about the stones called *There Was No Battle Here*.

I met curator Al Judson and he noted my interest in the numbers. He asked if I would like to archive the letters from a WWI soldier who was stationed at Sarcee Training Camp, and I agreed.

Archiving meant wearing white gloves and opening each delicate envelope, removing the fragile paper inside and typing the letter onto the computer.

The soldier's name was David Argo, a Scottish born Canadian soldier who settled in Calgary with his wife Mae and their two children.

My relationship with the Argo family began with the letters David wrote between 1915 until his death in no man's land on the front lines in 1917. David Argo was not the stereotypical rough and ready war-movie type of soldier. He was a family man and a farmer who felt it was his duty to cross the ocean to defend the Empire. In his letters he showed great compassion for his fellow soldiers, and also for the loss of life in the German ranks.

Every letter to Mae ended with a string of Xs meaning kisses to his wife and young family. I appreciated his sense of duty and I grieved as I typed his final letter to Mae. Archiving David's letters was profound. It occurred to me that I knew very little about the families of our fallen, from any war - until now. (Mae and David Argo - Photo Right)

Out of a sense of deep gratitude for their family's sacrifice, I took David's letters and the story of this Canadian settler to his descendants still living on the family farm called Tillymaud, in Scotland. I had written songs based on his letters and I sang them to the students in school concerts in the Aberdeen district where David was raised. I was impressed to see a memorial bearing a long list of names of local boys who had emigrated and served in another country's army. Carved in stone, the list included 'Canadians' David and his brother Alex Argo. It was a remarkable tribute that even though their 'sons' had emigrated, they would never be forgotten.

I confess that prior to learning about the Stones of Signal Hill I didn't want to wade into war topics. I didn't understand the lure of metal and smoke, artillery and ammo, or how one human could kill another. Nor did I understand the 'calling' to become a soldier. I didn't grow up with war so I didn't think it affected me. But David and Mae Argo did affect me. And so did the Isfelds.

In early 2005 I was volunteering at TMM singing for the students who were learning about Canada's role in the world wars. Al Judson wrapped up his educational presentation on WWI and everyone joined in singing the final chorus of *There Was No Battle Here*. We left the theatre and I decided to walk through the exhibit halls before going home. The museum is a fascinating place, but it is also a sobering experience to read about the events and artefacts identified with death and suffering.

As I walked around a corner something caught my eye. I did a double take. Was that a doll I saw on the wall? Encased in glass was a crocheted doll with a blue beret. Even though he was faceless, the colourful little guy was still charming. I remember feeling a shift in my emotions, from solemn to cheerful. I was smiling. I asked what this doll was doing in a war museum and the education director at the time, Carolyn Foard, told me it was an Izzy Doll and then said, "Phyllis, you have to meet the Isfelds."

I began a correspondence with the Isfelds in January of 2006. Brian and Carol were interested in the poetry and music I'd written about the stones of Calgary's Signal Hill and David and Mae Argo. It seemed to suffice as a calling card and they were both eager to tell me about Mark and the progress of the Izzy Doll project.

A few months later I visited the Isfelds at their home in Courtney B.C. The following year, when Brian came to Calgary for the Peacekeeper ceremony, he brought a package of discs he had prepared. We sat at my computer viewing his family photographs, Mark's letters, catalogued images of Brian's hobbies, historical badges, pins, rocks, and gemstones, and Carol's beautiful ceramics and paintings. For two hours we scrolled through what seemed like an Isfeld family presentation. I was fascinated by everything, but I remember wondering why he was showing me all of this. An inner voice said, 'just listen.' So I did. Brian told me to keep the discs. I didn't think about it again until two years later.

During the time we had corresponded, Brian and Carol had taught me about the families of our fallen soldiers and the unique issues they faced. Just before Carol died I felt an urgency to switch from another project to record a music CD that would bring attention to these remarkable families. Called *In Harm's Way*, it included a sixteen-page booklet which I had asked Brian to edit. He did a great job and by mid November the album was released. By the end of November Brian had been diagnosed with cancer. It was terminal and he died just months after Carol.

The reason for the urgency I had felt to produce *In Harm's Way* became clear after Carol and Brian passed away. *My Son Our Sons,* which Carol wrote, and my songs *The Izzy Doll* and the single *In Harm's Way* were all on the album. (Brian had asked me to write about Boomer, another brave soldier included in this book, as a surprise for his mother, Maureen.) I thought everything that needed to be said had been said.

Fast-forward two years to 2009. I received an email from someone concerned about an article in a newspaper about the Izzy Doll, wherein the facts were inaccurate. I thought, "Oh, great, another piece of Canadian history that's going to be lost." Then I remembered the stack of discs Brian had given me. It was the Isfelds' history waiting to be written down. It was clear that someone had to preserve their story — and it looked as though I was the candidate.

Phyllis Wheaton
Calgary 2011

Dedicated to

This book is dedicated to the hands behind the knitting needles and crochet hooks, mothers and grandmothers, great-grandmothers, knitters groups and students and others who have, as of July 2011, created over one million Izzy Dolls for the children of war and the poorest of the poor.

Your intent for peace is being felt throughout the world.

CHAPTER 1

MASTER CORPORAL MARK ROBERT ISFELD
BORN AUGUST 14, 1962 KILLED JUNE 21, 1994

An Izzy Doll

Mark

Kelly and Mark

Mark in Kuwait

EARLY YEARS

"Ideas of peace, justice, international cooperation and altruism are commonly used to describe Peacekeepers and Canadians as a people as well."
- Excerpt from a conference paper on Peacekeeping presented
by PhD candidate Colin McCullough

Children have a natural affinity for tales of adventure and Mark Isfeld's Icelandic lineage, complete with warriors and heroes on both sides of the family, fed his inner boy's craving for excitement.

Within the proud chapters of the family memoirs, there was a great uncle who served in the Boer War in South Africa, and another great uncle who left his dairy farm in Gimli, Manitoba, to serve in WWI with the 197th Vikings, a regiment formed from Scandinavian Manitobans. Other relatives who enlisted during the second great war included a tail gunner who flew a Lancaster Bomber, a WWII tank commander, and several army infantry and artillery soldiers who were directly involved in the liberation of Holland. Some returned home to resume their lives, but many remained, buried in Canadian War Cemeteries on a distant continent, having played a part in restoring freedom and ending a world war. Equally compelling were the Nordic tales of mythological characters. Mark grew up with the stories of Odin, the God of wisdom, victory, war and death who commanded magic, poetry and prophecy at whim and received the souls of the warriors at his table in Valhalla, the hall of the fallen.

It is understandable how Mark's family history and the lure of Scandinavian mythology could have sparked a little boy's fantasy about warriors. He did become a soldier. But it was his inherent idealism nurtured by a family and a society who valued fundamental rights and freedoms that determined the type of soldier he actually became.

Mirroring a respect for the written word instilled by his parents and grandparents, particularly his paternal grandfather, Arilius, Mark had written home throughout his adult life. It is because of the copious amounts of correspondence, prose, and poetry left behind by Mark and his elders that the stories in this book can be documented.

Mark's mother, Carol, had saved every one of his letters; many years after his death they remain the last tangible link to his thoughts and opinions. His father, Brian, took on the emotionally draining responsibility of typing all Mark's letters into what he called an "anthology that reflected his life." This is Brian's introduction to his son:

"Mark Robert Isfeld was born in Zweibrucken, Germany, 14 August, 1962. The second of three boys granted us. He was a pudgy-faced bundle of energy. We were living in the town of Contwig, Germany, a result of my being transferred to 3 (Fighter) Wing, Royal Canadian Air Force in June of 1962. Contwig is a picturesque little farming village close by the Air Base in Zweibrucken. Mark grew up in Contwig under the influence of our German neighbours and other military families living in the same area, mostly Canadian and American Service people. He attended German kindergarten and on our repatriation to Canada in 1967 spoke German as well as, or better than English." In July 1967, the Isfeld family was repatriated to the Royal Canadian Air Force base in Greenwood, Nova Scotia, the province where Mark spent his adolescent years.

"He attended school first at Dwight Ross School, located in the permanent married quarters in Greenwood. From July 1971 until December 1973 he attended Woodlawn Elementary in Dartmouth, Nova Scotia, where we had been transferred to 880 Squadron, Shearwater. His final years were at Middleton Nova Scotia Technical School, graduating in the spring of 1980. While in Middleton his focus was on welding, at which he became quite proficient.

"Mark, with his brothers, Leigh and Glenn, spent many joyous summer holidays with his paternal Grandparents (Arilius and Steinunn Isfeld) in Winnipeg, and his maternal Grandparents (George and Olina Donaldson) in Norwood, Ontario. When in Manitoba, much time was spent at Husavik, Manitoba on the shores of Lake Winnipeg and all three boys enjoyed being there immensely." Both sets of grandparents had lived through the Great Depression and World War II. They had witnessed incredible changes in Canada and in the world in communications, transportation, health and so much more. The values they passed on to their grandsons were practical and community-based principles — tools for survival: Make do with what you have and help when there is a need.

"Afflicted with the natural wanderlust of the young, Mark made his first thrust into the world of self-sufficiency by going to Winnipeg to look for work. He stayed with his paternal grandparents until he found an apartment of his own. He worked in Winnipeg about one year, then headed for Edmonton, Alberta, where the sequence of events leading up to this account of what should presumably have been an average life, began."

***

I had never met Mark Isfeld in person but I grew to know him through the stories of the people who knew him best and by reading the letters his mother had saved. His videos from his tours of duty, which he narrated, revealed an outgoing young man, interested in everything and everyone around him.

It seems Mark was destined to carry a torch for peace because he was the middle child, a birth order position which, as psychological research suggests, often produces the peacekeeper in a family. In fact, Mark's older brother, Leigh, speaks of his sibling as the peacekeeper in their family who owned a conscience of accountability, just like his mom.

He explains, "My brother was like my mom, both focused on situations or people or animals that were in need. Concerns most people would want to ignore. On a family holiday we saw a dog that had been hit by a car. My mom said, 'Ahhh that poor little dog'. It was painful to see and the dog was dying, and I thought there was nothing we could do. I wanted to walk away but my mom defended the dog's life right to the end, saying we had to help and at least try to find the family the suffering dog belonged to. On many occasions when she saw or heard something and sighed a big Ahhh of compassion I just knew, 'NOW who do we have to help?' But she was always right. And Mark was like that." As well as a heightened compassion for the suffering in the world, Mark and his mother shared an intuitive awareness. It was a spiritual antenna that reached across deserts and oceans, and as events would later attest, even after his death, from the other side. According to Leigh, his younger brother "was charismatic and had the girlfriends and he had the hugs that could make mom smile." Mark, he explains, was the quintessential 'parent' of a group, and willing to rise to the occasion to aid and support because it was the right thing to do, regardless of the obstacles.

Both Mark and his father had a love of history, antiques, and artefacts. In a letter to his pen pal Ken, Mark describes his interests:

All the books I read are historical in one way or another, from ancient to many favourite stories of the pioneers and fur traders. I also am a collector. I have many beautiful antiques from my bottle collection to old papers and other items of interest.

Leigh described Mark as "the best of both of our parents"; his mother's compassion and his dad's logic and reason. Mark could be business-like and tough when he needed to be but preferred to diffuse difficult situations by listening and talking, and often with humour. "Helping people was about Mom. Doing something about it was about Dad. Mark would say 'Do what you can, write a letter, then you can complain.'"

Leigh explained that his brother had a 'seventh sense.' "He was able to read a situation then poke you by saying the words that you were thinking but wouldn't say. And like our mother, he was most often right."

During Mark's early twenties, while working away from home, he wrote his parents frequently. In one letter he talked about making changes and becoming more serious about his future. An unplanned pregnancy with a former girlfriend had led to an adoption at birth, which one relative described as a difficult decision but an unselfish act that would give the baby hope for a promising future. With decided determination to make changes in his life, Mark dropped bad habits that were affecting his ability to focus and move forward. While working as a welder in Edmonton he wrote to his parents, who were living on Vancouver Island by then, about his inner struggle for a direction:

I want to do something substantial in my life and don't quite know how to go about it. I think I am starting to be a little more aware of myself and feel I could learn anything I put my mind to. Regardless, I want to go back to school; I'm not sure how or what. I'm going to try and join the Forces.

A subsequent letter told the story of how he made it into the military, not by luck, but by providence and perseverance. Mark's dream choice was Field Engineer; however he was unsuccessful with his first attempt in March 1986. Three weeks later he went back to talk to the captain about other options available to him, like Aero Engine, Air Frame, or Artillery. The captain appeared pleased to see Mark and commented, "Funny you should show up today, I wanted to talk to you." He explained that Mark was a prime candidate and that, "We haven't had an opening for ten months in Field Engineer. We got one today, and if you would still be willing, I'm going to ask the sergeant to offer you the position." To be offered a career as a Field Engineer, the job he was hoping for, was a sign that his aspirations were within reach. Basic training would begin in May with 24 weeks in Cornwallis, Nova Scotia, then on to Canadian Forces School of Military Engineering (CFSME) in Chilliwack, British Columbia.

Authors Note: A few years after the adoption, Mark had a dream about the baby. He posted his name in an adoption registry in the event she would search for him when she was older. When she came of age, Alisha did search for him. The trail led her to Mark's parents and the discovery that her father had died years earlier. Carol and Brian were ecstatic at the reunion with their granddaughter.

Glenn, Carol, Alisha, Brian, and Leigh at The Wall of Honour, Peacekeepers Park, Calgary Alberta

BASIC TRAINING

Well, I have got millions of tidbits I could share but as you can see I'm snafu. I'll write something coherent when I get my kit finished. Right now I only have time to be tired and severely frustrated! I love it. I wish I had done it when I was younger. It is demanding yet satisfying. It is a good feeling to just put my "362 Isfeld" on everything. I want bad to succeed. It's tough!!

- Mark's comments about basic training

Basic training is a mechanism that dares privates to measure up, challenging their physical and mental endurance. Gruelling repetition, combat drills, and endless inspections are part of the routine and a necessary priming to build soldiers. At the height of the intensity of training, most recruits are convinced they are being tormented at the hands of sadists who delight in their suffering. The truth is that basic training methodology has been deliberately and intelligently scripted to affect an outcome; a strong unwavering soldier who can be expected to get the job done under the most demanding circumstances. Cadets who succeed and graduate speak of the personal pride they have gained and the pride they feel for their fellow graduates. No one ever said it would be easy, and for Mark the challenge was part of the attraction.

Well, yes this is everything and more than it is cracked up to be. Head games. They give you so much to remember. You are frustrated because they don't give you time to do it: Just freaking out, then they give you more and you don't just have to have it done; it has to be perfect!

Inadequate time limits force predictable mistakes. Obedience without question and compliance to the chain of command are primary objectives of the instructors. Mistakes or the smallest infraction from being late to a wrinkled shirt or complaining about an order could mean a loss of privileges. Hard-nosed instructors are viewed as the enemy, so cadets band together out of self-preservation. This bonding helps turn them into a tight and effective unit.

And always they have surprises like inspection on the first day we wear our uniform. The Master Corporal gives us only one-half hour instruction on dress and the shaping of berets and next morning we have a Master Corporal and a Petty Officer screaming and spitting in our face. They gave us 60 or 70 things to label and they were tearing people's tags off. One guy started to argue and the shit hit the fan! It's yes or no.

Team work, the foundation of effective soldiering, is taught immediately. It may be a surprise to a cadet (but not to their mothers) that when everyone pitches in, even mundane housekeeping tasks are made easier and dealt with faster.

We have a platoon of 140 and it is broken down alphabetically into four squads, one platoon senior, and four squad leaders… This morning we cleaned up the drill hall. It is amazing what 140 guys can do in a short time when they work as a team… We have all helped each other out and ironed, sewn, swept, polished, mopped, and set up.

Mark gained a reputation for his positive attitude, his kid-like smile, and the levity he continually injected into serious moments. On a particularly rigorous training day, he resigned himself to the inevitable without losing his sense of humour.

I'm sore. Today was a really physical one. Drill was like PT and PT was unbelievable. I did about 300 push-ups, about 150 sit-ups and countless squat thrusts. To start PT class I came out into the gym jogging and I had forgotten to take my keys off so I ran up to the Corporal and asked if I could do fifty? He found that amusing and said "that's the spirit."

"Anyone who joins the military better have a sense of humour," was the belief of Mark's dad, an RCAF veteran who knew from experience that laughter was a reliable release from mounting tensions. In fact laughter is a physiological stress reliever — a natural built-in medication without side effects, just benefits. As well, comic relief and pranks cement a soldier's boots in the anecdotal history of their troop.

Holy snappin!! I would have written sooner, but as it stands I don't know which way to turn. I don't dare sleep in my bed because I would never have time to make it up in the morning. We have to shave every morning, as well as clean our bed space, measure our locker, foot locker and bed. Polish our boots and make sure we are dressed properly, that is: boots tied regulation, laces tucked, combats bloused, combat shirt sleeves folded absolutely perfect, all in about 25 minutes… Time out. OK, it's well after lights out. Most guys can't sleep; some who are, are talking in their sleep; the guys two bunks over are bugging this guy in his sleep while he's talking, saying "Colin, it's mom." "Come get your Cheerios." So he says; "It's not breakfast time yet mom." We are splitting a gut!

Mark said he had no regrets joining the military. The bar was high and he sounded determined to reach it.

Mark did succeed; he graduated from basic training in Cornwallis, Nova Scotia. He was pumped at the prospect of entering the next stage of his career — seventeen weeks at the CFSME (Canadian Forces School of Military Engineering) at the opposite end of the country in Chilliwack, British Columbia.

Training as a Field Engineer, Mark's education encompassed mine warfare and demolitions, building bridges, and operating heavy equipment. Now living in the same province as his parents there was no written correspondence within this time period. Happily they visited often over the phone and face to face. Mark could also devote more attention to civilian relationships now, and a certain girl named Kelly had caught his eye.

"The business of a soldier is to be either fighting a war or preparing for one if they are doing anything else, they are defrauding the public."

Brigadier General "Kip" Kirby

After graduating from CFSME, soldiers were assigned to a Combat Engineer Regiment. Fortunately for Mark, he was designated to 1 Combat Engineers Regiment (1CER) based in Chilliwack, which meant he didn't have to relocate. The engineers continued to train and gel as a cohesive unit. Reliance and trust as well as friendships developed over the months, forming a tight brotherhood.

Mark's commanding officer, Major (later Major-General) Ed Fitch, got to know Mark personally as they were both on the 1CER shooting team. Honing their skills and preparing for eventual opportunities in the theatre of war was the focus of 1CER over the next few years. Ed explains the process of skill building during this interval.

"Since there was no war that we were called to in the period 1985-88, we used the time in an annual cycle of training that brought the regiment to a peak of fighting efficiency by Spring /early Summer of each year. Training would progress from individual skills through building cohesive teams at the section, troop, squadron, regiment, and brigade/ division levels in succession. Some of the highlights were the two 'bridge gallops' we did in the Pemberton-Harrison-Chilliwack corridor, winter training on the Chilcotin Plateau, and the annual brigade/division concentrations in Wainwright and Suffield. Sports were woven into the programme to help maintain mental and physical health."

***

Phone calls and visits to his family were regular during this time. On fishing jaunts, Mark and his dad would talk shop, politics, and history. Fun loving and affirming like his mother, Mark was interested in her latest art projects and reading her most recent poetry. He had a genuine desire to hear what both his parents had to say and many a night they sat around the dinner table after one of Carol's famous spaghetti suppers in serious discussion. It is a universal hope of parents to see their adult children find a suitable partner. Brian recounts the next major life change for his middle son. "After leaving Cornwallis, and while stationed in Chilliwack, Mark met and fell deeply in love with Kelly Lemaster, his wife to be. Kelly is an American who lived in Everson, Washington, just across the border from the Chilliwack area. Kelly has two children, Kari and Wade Gardener by a previous marriage. Mark gave them the love and understanding he was so capable of."

Prior to their marriage, Mark was posted to Kuwait on a UN Peacekeeping mission. Not only was it Mark's first experience on an overseas mission in a danger zone, it was a test of his fiancée's emotional endurance. Being in love with a soldier on another continent and trying to organize their December wedding while worlds apart was a test of wills and their love.

Sir, more than kisses, letters mingle souls; for, thus friends absent, speak.

John Donne

Letter writing dates back thousands of years. It may be considered old fashioned, even a dying art to many people today but for a soldier deployed to a foreign land, a letter from home can sustain morale and boost mental wellbeing. Mark was already a seasoned letter writer, but once deployed letter writing became a vital link for him as well as his loved ones. It was not uncommon to see one-liners tucked into his letters such as *It's hard to impress upon people the meaning of 'mail in the field'* emphasising the importance of receiving mail. For Mark, receiving mail was *good when you do, bad when you don't.*

A letter with his name on it was an umbilical cord to the latest news, gossip and updates from home. For Mark, mail opened a sentimental window through which encouragement and love flowed, especially during difficult times: *Well it surely is nice to have your name called at mail call. I appreciate the encouragement also, especially now we are in one of the toughest weeks…*

Hooking up with loved ones a continent away was not easy, even with the 1990's technology. Making a telephone call often meant waiting in long line-ups for your turn. Even when there was a lack of stationery supplies Mark was not deterred from keeping in touch. He made do with what he had, using whatever he could find to write on to get his message out. His parents, fiancée, aunts and uncles, grandparents and godparents, and friends sent a trail of encouragement with their words. Ken Johnson, a stranger who wanted to support our troops, offered to correspond with 'any soldier.' Ken's first letter resulted in a pen-pal relationship that lasted for the duration of Mark's three tours.

Besides letters everyone sent gifts that were as precious as gold nuggets in the mailbag; books, magazines, fresh garden peppers, tollhouse cookies and socks from Mom, and even fish from Dad. Conversely, Mark was eager to please and relished the 'hunt' to fill requests from home. Coins, stamps, rocks, photos, even sweaters or T-shirts from exotic locations he visited on leave were checked off his shopping list.

Letters flowed back and forth throughout his three tours of duty in foreign lands. Writing home was a release valve as he shared his adventures under a myriad of both routine and complex political circumstances. He vented his exasperation about the conditions surrounding him and expressed his frustrations of the job, as well as his accomplishments. It was therapeutic, while keeping family and friends attuned to his situation. His letters were also indicators of his mood and how he was handling the mounting stress. Mark's earliest letters in Kuwait began with a curious and positive tone, but as the months progressed his frustration at the predicament of the innocent and his sense of inadequacy to help became more evident.

Certain phrases were telltale of the mounting pressure and on several occasions he had begun to outline a particularly graphic scene then ended abruptly with *enough of that.* Perhaps as the words formed on the paper he realized he should spare his loved ones the grisly details. Or perhaps he had to spare himself reliving the memory.

The fact of the matter was that mail in both directions was a lifeline for a soldier, and as Mark said, *It sure makes the day when mail comes in.*

FIRST UN PEACEKEEPING MISSION KUWAIT

"we only need to look at what we are really doing in the world and at home and we'll know what it is to be canadian."

Adrienne Clarkson

Between 1990 and 1991 more than 4,000 Canadian forces participated in a coalition force led by the United States to push invading Iraq out of Kuwait. A ceasefire in March 1991 saw elated Kuwaiti people grateful for the restoration of their independence. UN peacekeeping efforts continued after the cease-fire which, according to the Veterans Affairs web site, involved monitoring the demilitarized zone between the two countries, investigating cease fire violations, and clearing landmines.

In April 1991 Mark was deployed on his first peacekeeping mission. He would implement his skills in mine detection and clearing and demolition of uxons as he worked alongside his 1CER brothers. Brian had observed that his son's departure was one of anticipation and exuberance, which was a normal reflex for a young soldier who had spent years in preparation and was ready for adventure.

***

As Mark's plane flew over Kuwait he was stunned at the vast expanse of desert and the wind-shaped drifts that owned the landscape. Deathly black clouds foreshadowed a spectacle he described this way: *The desert was something else from the air. So different; when we got over Kuwait it was unreal. Like nothing I've ever seen. There was fire everywhere, like giant smoky torches burning indiscriminately. Everywhere there was smoke; black, grey, thick like huge rain clouds.*

Back home in Canada the CBC reported the burning fields in Kuwait; more than 700 oil wells had been set ablaze by the retreating Iraqi army at Suddam Hussein's command. For Mark's parents it was difficult to imagine, even with the video footage on television. From Mark's perspective from the air and on the ground, it was shocking. The polluting oil wells burned for more than eight months before finally being extinguished; the resulting environmental devastation is still an issue today. As well as contaminating the soil and water, the pollution caused respiratory related illnesses to the local population and the soldiers stationed there.

During his first weeks in Kuwait, Mark wrote about the difficulties of adapting to the desert environment. He was shocked at how physically exhausting it was to perform his duties in temperatures upwards of 45 degrees Celsius. *It is like opening an oven and getting the hot blast in your face — 'cause the wind always blows and it blows hot! And you sweat like a madman and feel so tired.* It is a big effort to do anything. It took days to acclimatize to the sweltering heat that could easily provoke throbbing headaches. He said he was thankful for an *abundant supply of water, good medics and pills to ease headaches from dehydration.*

The howling winds were a challenge, too; they assaulted his face with dust, forcing him to be constantly rubbing or picking at his eyes, a habit that continued for months after his return home to Canada. Another natural environmental challenge was avoiding the local reptiles and arachnids, some poisonous and some just pesky. Scorpions, snakes, lizards and camel spiders (with teeth) made the Canadian mosquito look like a house pet by comparison. Mark said he was keen to meet one of each just for the experience.

Mark could accept nature's uniqueness in this part of the world, but he found it difficult to come to terms with the man-made devastation. It was to be expected that they would see evidence of the Iraqi invasion and signs of battle, but the degree of destruction and metal carnage was astounding — the desert landscape had been transformed into a veritable combat graveyard.

Again a day to remember. We went to Ummqasar to the hovercraft site. On the way there, we drove through the killing field, and it stunk! Stunk! Of death. A most terrible stench as you can imagine. The destruction was awesome close up. Tanks, APC's, cars, trucks, full of holes, piled up, burned, upside down — unreal!! I also got to see the burning oil fields even closer than before; it makes you really sick to see it. I counted 68 wells in one and 52 in another, and those are just what you can see on the outside because of the smoke!

I saw Iraqi defences that blew my mind. Trenches and bunkers all full of rocket-propelled grenades and ammo everywhere. They just picked up and left. I saw bunkers and aircraft hangars that were bombed, as well as buildings that were totalled. We flew right over that section of road that was devastated. There were hundreds of vehicles burned and bombed... Anyway this whole country is a massive defensive position. I could not believe it. The news doesn't show what I saw!

The predicament of the children caught in the war's aftermath was unsettling, and the contrast to a Canadian childhood was painfully obvious. At times the children's irrepressible cheerfulness was contradictory to their living conditions, then in an instant the mask would come off as starvation reduced their moods to competitive desperation.

We drove through one of the refugee camps and it was terrible. But all the little kids came running and waved. All the people seemed really happy to see us. The little kids run top speed in bare feet!! Over glass and rocks and metal!!

They wave and laugh hysterically, it's a good feeling, and like being in a parade that is miles and miles long. The kids in Iraq I felt more sorry for cause they are not in a good way, living in decrepit buildings with garbage everywhere and they are starving. We were throwing our rations to them. It was quite a sight as they would ask us for food, pointing to their mouth or stomach but still all smiles. They wanted our water as much as food. There were two little boys who came out that we gave some food to. Very good feeling until he went back to the crowd. Some other children chased the crap out of him to take it.

Orders came down to refrain from giving food to the refugee children. The higher-ups were concerned that children swarming the military vehicles for handouts and fighting over the food could get injured or killed, which then would jeopardize the soldiers' reputation with the locals. Mark wrote of the women who were as hungry as the kids. It was an impossibility to try to ignore the needs of the starving.

I saw a little boy being pulled by his brother on a makeshift cart. The little boy had no legs. Also there were kids on crutches all over, and bandaged kids missing feet and arms. It's no wonder. A little boy about eight years old came up to a guy when we were clearing an area and he was all smiles holding a live grenade!

Scene after scene of amputee children hobbling through the streets haunted Mark. Many had been dismembered by a landmine encounter, or maimed when curiously handling a bomb as though it was a toy. It was commonplace for a child to find a stash of explosive devices and run to a respected soldier with their 'find' for approval and attention. These events anchored Mark's belief that Sappers, demining and eliminating stockpiles of dangerous explosives, saved lives and reduced the potential for tragedy.

Traveling within the region was a strange experience. Referring to his first foray onto the highway Mark commented, *It's funny how you can slip right in and sort of enjoy the "no rules" driving; no cops, and speed limit signs ignored.* He told of how an Arab driver had pulled up beside him at a light listening to "Allah's Top Ten" and it made him smile thinking that *they were no different than us listening to music in our cars.*

18

It wasn't long before the novelty of no-holds-barred driving wore off. There were several close calls and at one point Mark described five Arab vehicles abreast on a two-lane road, traveling 70 to 80 miles per hour. *I was more worried about making it back alive in that truck than I could be in any minefield.* He concluded that *the Arabs were the worst drivers on the face of the earth!!* (The exclamation marks belong to Mark.)

It had been the anniversary of Mark's fifth year in the army and he made a note of what he did that day — a trip to another refugee camp. Mark described it as a disgusting place where feeble makeshift shelters were erected from sticks of wood and whatever the people could find. One little boy tapped into Mark's feelings of patriotism: *Little kids were bringing us mortars, grenades and rockets. We kept telling them to stop but they won't listen. They want our attention so badly. One little boy came up to me and poked me in the chest and said, "Merica? Merica?" I said "No, Canada," and he proudly walked around to the rest of our guys saying "Canada," "Canada," and shaking their hand.*

Orphaned by war, starvation or illness, Mark saw the children as innocent victims with great needs apart from the mandate the soldiers were there to address. Disease spread through refugee camps where poor nutrition, lack of water, sanitation, and medical support allowed disease to run rampant. *All of them ask for water or food… There were people in bad shape all over and some guys said they saw some bodies. . . One little boy walked up to a guy and said "Mista my mudda die." I saw a bunch of kids on the road fighting, just slugging it out... I made about 30 trips back and forth through Ummqasar. And I'm sick and tired of driving past little kids begging for water and food. You can't give because you'd have a riot.*

Mark's brother Leigh, retells a story that a soldier from 1CER told him about how Mark had a way of holding people accountable. A bunch of kids were swarming the Peacekeepers, as they often did, hoping for any kind of treats. Mark dug into his pockets and began giving out candies. He looked over at his buddy and said, "Don't you have any candy?" The soldier replied, "Yeah, but I only have a couple and look how many kids there are." At this, Mark challenged him, "So you're going to leave them in your pocket and make yourself feel better? Do what you can with what you got." That was Mark, the soldier explained, the company's conscience who held his troop to task, especially when it came to the children.

It seemed surreal to Mark that his home in Canada had all the comforts known to man and yet these children had nothing. He wrote about the look of desperation on the children's faces, and he had sharp criticism for Canadians who take their peace and abundance for granted.

After what I've seen, people better be careful when they complain about a lack of something, or say "I need." We take far too much for granted. I know, I've seen looks on some little children's faces I'll never forget.

It was the contrast between our two nations that opened Mark's eyes to what he had taken for granted about his own country. Returning to Kuwait after a leave at home, Mark writes about his appreciation for Canada's simple beauties and his frustration for the people of this struggling nation.

I just came back here from leave in Canada last week and I will never take for granted again our beautiful country. I noticed the sweet smelling air the most, and I stood out in the rain and walked barefoot in the grass. Truly we are blessed. I feel so sorry for the people here. They are so ignorant, scratching out an existence from the dust while their leaders spend all their money on Arms.

***

Mark's compassion extended towards anyone, including Iraqi soldiers who were often victims as well. On his way back from Doha to pick up a truck, Mark passed through a check stop. *When I got to the Iraq border, one of the border guards stopped me and meekly asked if I could give him something to eat, but I didn't have any rations at all. I asked him if he would like a bottle of water and he gratefully accepted. It made me feel kind of sorry for him even if he was the enemy. I'm here on a peacekeeping mission and all soldiers have an affinity for hardship.*

A collage of imagery emerged from Mark's letters that might describe the end of an intense day in the field. Retreating to his living space only a thin wall separated the chaotic world outside from the comfort of his memories. Laying on his cot, visions of his wife

scanning for landmines

to be, and yearnings for her, swirled about his thoughts. He bit into a spicy tollhouse cookie his mom had sent and thought about home. In a mind-video he saw his dad in a wooden two-man boat, fishing the sea for a prospective grand catch. He saw himself sitting in the boat too. "Next trip home," he had written. With the last bite of his cookie he imagined his mother's face and how her heart was strained fearing for his safety. The stress his family felt in his absence was yet another issue that left him with feelings of helplessness.

Mark couldn't let Mother's Day go unnoticed. Even though he was many time zones away, it was an opportunity to remind his mother of his deep respect and love. No stationery or paper supplies were available, so he made do with a cereal box and designed a card with a poem. It was one of his mother's most cherished gifts. It read:

> *Happy Mother's Day Mom! No rain! No snow! No sleet!*
> *Just dust and desert heat;*
> *No matter how my brain gets burned*
> *I won't forget The most important thing I've learned*
>
> *I love you. With "warm" thoughts*
> *Mark of Arabia.*

Kuwait had been an adventure that satiated Mark's taste for excitement, but it had served up much more. Mark had written that Peacekeepers were not being given the sort of shelter and equipment they needed. He recognized a disconnect between Canadians and their soldiers and felt that public opinion was reflected in the politicians' pocketbooks. He was certain that if everyone heard the stories and the results of their work as Peacekeepers, support would be stronger.

It is seldom that we in the Canadian Forces see the approval of the citizens of Canada. More often, we see the negatives, like people wanting to cut budgets, close bases, or cut personnel. I think that if we got more press and the people felt more a part of us we would have the kind of support that ensures a soldier that someone cares about the sacrifices we all make.

Kuwait had been Mark's training ground. Four-and five-day bivouacs (no frill camping in a region that was hardly cottage country) challenged him. Beholding the shocking aftermath of war and its victims struggling to survive in the refugee camps changed him. Witnessing the direct consequences of landmines and explosive devices that mutilated and killed increased his dedication to save lives.

Preparing for his return home, Mark summed up his Middle East experience in one line: *This tour has been a "BIG" part in my life, opening my eyes to things I never imagined.* And he ended the letter with his usual optimism. *I'm going to do my laundry now. We have to do it by hand. Not fun. But it sure dries quickly!*

Cool autumn winds blew gently against Mark's tanned cheeks like welcoming kisses. He stepped onto the tarmac into Canada's changing season with a big grin on his face. It was telling of his eagerness to embrace his fiancée and reunite with his family. But his beaming smile could also have been for the gratefulness for what was absent. No sweltering heat or dust, no signs of war or starving children, or street kids without limbs. And no spiders with teeth. He was home.

Life between tours of duty was a period of adjustment and a time to de-stress and settle back into the abundance of Canada and what Mark called *our own lovely kind of chaos*. This was not a simple task. Mark's conscience could not let him forget the stark images of the Middle East. Leigh recalls a conversation after the homecoming when he observed his brother's comments and expressions.

Mark was frustrated and concerned for the innocent who had to live with their lot in Kuwait while he could board a plane and return to his life in Canada. The lenses of his rose-colored glasses were dulled by greater truths. Now home, he could not pretend that all was right with the world. He knew different. Leigh said he was wounded — emotionally. Although it was comforting to see his family and friends, Mark carried a backpack full of memories and images that would take some time to find a place to store. And the baggage would increase with his next tour.

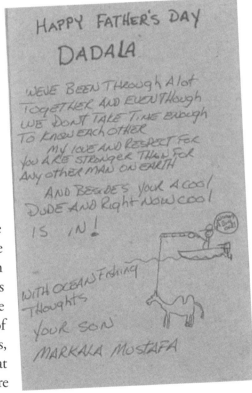

HAPPY FATHER'S DAY
DADALA

WE'VE BEEN THROUGH A lot TOGETHER AND EVEN THOUGH WE DON'T TAKE TIME ENOUGH TO KNOW EACH OTHER
MY love AND RESPECT FOR YOU ARE STRONGER THAN FOR ANY OTHER MAN ON EARTH
AND BESIDES YOUR A COOL DUDE AND Right NOW COOL IS IN!

WITH OCEAN FISHING Thoughts
YOUR SON
MARKALA MOSTAFA

Mark and Kelly's upcoming wedding would be stressful too, but the happy kind of stress. Deciding to marry in December, close to Christmas and Kelly's birthday, had been a strategic plan. The military tried to be accommodating by coinciding leave time with special occasions, so it was Mark's idea to arrange their special dates close together to optimize their chance of being together. In the "anthology" about his son's life, Brian wrote: "All was not a bed of roses, due to the complexities of American /Canadian customs laws, and the fact that Mark was a serviceman with the obligations that go along with this profession. But love conquered all and they were married on 20 December 1991."

The young couple settled into their new life. Mark continued training and taking courses. Approximately ten months after their wedding he was readying to leave on his second tour of duty. Besides the military paperwork, there was a will to update, power of attorney, and other matters he had to consider in case he was injured or killed. Few other occupations required facing these hard cold facts before setting off to work.

Mark's father noted: "There was no apprehension, just a feeling that he was on his way to another war torn area and knew the dangers and sights he would probably behold in this part of the world."

The exuberance he had shown for his first tour of duty was replaced with focused professionalism. His sense of excitement for the next adventure was now tempered by experience.

Leigh, Mark and Glenn

SECOND UN PEACEKEEPING MISSION CROATIA

"It was an attempt to confront and defeat the worst in Man with the best in Man, to counter violence with tolerance, might with moderation, and war with peace."

Kofi A. Annan, United Nations Secretary-General (1998)
speaking about the first UN Peacekeeping mission

The dissolution of Yugoslavia saw a divided population attempting to gain independence by forming their own countries. Some were successful with relatively little conflict; however, for Croatia it was quite the opposite.

Like the Serbs, Croatian leaders also had a vision for an ethnically pure country and sanctioned the process of 'ethnic cleansing' where their army would advance into a territory and expel civilians of other ethnicities to create a 'pure' enclave for their own people. It was a system practised in the former Yugoslavia by both Croats and Serbs, as war crime tribunals would evidence in the years to come.

Families who had been established in these regions for centuries were tortured and slaughtered, homes were burned to the ground, and an exodus of hundreds of thousands fled to neighbouring European countries as political refugees.

The European Community intervened but was unable to stop the bloodshed and the wave of displaced refugees. They requested assistance from the UN, which organized the United Nations Protection Force (UNPROFOR), the first of several peacekeeping efforts. UNPROFOR was composed of troops from forty countries. Peacekeepers were to monitor the tenuous cease-fire lines and deliver humanitarian aid to the victims caught within the territories under siege.

Standard UN Peacekeeping policy dictated deployment after warring parties had agreed to a cease-fire. But in this case neither side was in agreement, so the Peacekeepers presence was viewed with contempt. Mark was aware of the fragile situation in Croatia. Under the UN rules of engagement, Peacekeepers could not fire unless fired upon. He knew he was stepping into an ambiguous role where some said they were going in to keep the peace where there was no peace to keep. In Kuwait the Peacekeepers were welcomed by the people, but in Croatia, they were viewed with suspicion and even hostility.

Brian explained that Mark's job as a Sapper in the former Yugoslavia was predominantly clearing the roads of mines to allow their troops to move without obstruction or accident. They would also clear property and buildings of landmines so civilians and farmers could try to resume their livelihoods. In theory, warring sides are required to map the location of landmines they have seeded. In an eventual cease-fire, landmines could then be easily located and destroyed. However, in Croatia sometimes maps were not kept at all, and those that existed were not always accurate or had been misplaced. As well, the Canadians suspected that hostile characters might re-seed cleared land, so even supposedly safe zones were suspect.

24

Surveying and the sweeping of suspect land with metal detectors was meticulous work, which demanded total concentration. Once located, landmines could be detonated where they lay or diffused by hand, depending on the circumstances. Stashes of ordnance and uxons were stockpiled and destroyed under controlled detonation. Mark's tour in Kuwait had given him the experience he needed in his area of expertise. However, this would be the first time he would be clearing mines under combat conditions.

✳✳✳

Artists and writers have painted and written about the natural beauty of Croatia; miles of craggy coastline kissing crystal clear seas, scented pine forests, and the rugged Dinaric Alps with their fortress ruins exposing the evidence of centuries of war. In a letter to his godparents Mark described the countryside as breathtaking and beautiful. Writing his folks he made a comparison to Canada's coastal provinces where he had spent so much of his youth.

I've been here for six days now and it has rained every one. And when it rains it pours. It is really nice countryside. Every house is a little farm. It smells fresh too, for the most part. Sort of looks like a cross between B.C. and Nova Scotia.

The bucolic landscape idealized peace, but the warring humans were anything but peaceful. The Peacekeepers were not welcome here and almost daily they were scorned by the locals and the children who had been taught to shun them. *A little girl gave us the finger today, they just see us as soldiers, not as Peacekeepers. Locally there have been killings since I arrived. Terrorist style drive-by shootings, but only Serb-Croat. No one has directed any at us that I am aware of ... A town was taken by the Serbs a few days back. It was suspected that it was given up. Anyway 500 refugees were fleeing and being shelled. Sick eh?*

Having been raised in Canada, a country rooted in its ethnic diversity, Mark saw the intensity and acceptance of the hatred here and was repulsed by it. Ignoring the animosity of the locals, Mark accepted any opportunity to win their trust. Giving something, he had learned, was a positive gesture; kindness was understood in any language.

I took some pictures today of two real old men who were pulling a cart full of apples and some walnuts. When I approached them they seemed to be a little worried. I had my rifle. I gave them each a chocolate bar and they sure smiled then!

As they realized this Peacekeeper was no threat, the two old men shifted gears from fearing to friendly. But there was not enough time or chocolate to sway negative opinions one person at a time.

The delivery of humanitarian aid fell under the mandate of UNPROFOR and, as required, Peacekeepers would be sent to protect transportation routes disrupted by the actions of the warring forces. *As for news … we were almost sent to a bridge over the Sava River that the Serbs want closed to block humanitarian efforts. Well, it was going to stay open. We were ready to move and loaded. The carrier was just pulling out when the call came that it was solved with words.*

As Mark put it, it was solved with words. That was hopeful, but from his perspective at the time, prospects for this war-ravaged region looked grim. In the same letter he added that the anticipated casualties caused by the weather and fighting could be as high as 500,000.

* According to the Dept. of Public Information, United Nations, September 1996 because of the presence of UNPROFOR between November 1992 and January 1993, humanitarian aid reached an estimated 800,000 beneficiaries in 110 locations throughout Bosnia and Herzegovina.

✳✳✳

Occasionally during deployments, celebrities would make appearances. Generals and politicians inspected and followed the troops, often with fanfare attached. Mark wrote of his indifference to most of the VIP events, but there was one journalist from Chilliwack, B.C., who had earned special status in Mark's eyes. Andy Holota had embedded into 1CER's tours, following them and documenting their daily routine of his hometown regiment.

Initially he was motivated by the excitement of the adventure and was keen to hone his journalistic skills, but he said 1CER grew on him. "1CER was 'my' unit. I had worked with them on community projects, participated in (and) covered several combat engineer training exercises in the interior of B.C. and Alberta, and finally, when they went into a war theatre, I wanted to cover them."

He did more than cover 'his' unit. Through Andrew's initiative, endorsed by the British Columbia newspaper *Chilliwack Progress*, he gave presentations to the families of the 1CER, showing 1CER at work encompassing the risks and achievements. Andrew said the families of these soldiers were extremely grateful for the insights and thanked him personally.

Mark and Andy had met several times both in Canada and during Mark's tours of duty. A friendship had forged, as often happens when forces draw people together as allies with a common purpose.

Mark had written a letter to Andy that he may have intended for a larger audience. Descriptive and passionate, Mark speaks of his impressions of Croatia, of the impact of war on the innocent. He writes of the importance of the Peacekeepers' presence to save lives and recognized the emotional burden of families of soldiers whose love and support was paramount. Mark's letter follows in its entirety.

oct 92 camp Polom, Croatia

Last year, while I was still in Kuwait, my wife Kelly and I finalized plans for our marriage. At first she insisted we have a summer wedding. I explained to her that a christmas wedding would be better for us. since her birthday is Dec 27, that would practically ensure I would always be home for our anniversary. This year our first anniversary will be shared together only because my warrant officer insisted my leave time be changed. I will come back to croatia on my wife's birthday. we will share our first anniversary and christmas together. Two out of three ain't bad!

From my eyes croatia is a terrible scar on a once beautiful face. I have seen churches possibly 500 years old in ruins. A monastery with breathtaking architecture; fruit trees and grape vines fill a courtyard where human voices are gone. I can almost imagine priests gathering grapes to make wine for their communion. The church has a tall steeple with a stunning mosaic on the front. A clock hangs from the other side, but time has stopped for this ancient, sacred place of worship. Devils of war have made this treasure of history a worthless eyesore.

My heart was torn from my chest today. I saw a helpless old lady on the porch of an apartment. she was the only resident. People with larger interests than the life of a pathetic old woman stormed through her town and tore her life away. They ruined all her possessions, forcing her to scrounge for utensils. I wonder if she will survive the winter?

One day, I can't help but wonder: where are all the people? There is a strange emptiness; peoples' hours of labour, all their skill and love that went into building homes; some have been handed down through countless generations. They lie in ruined piles of brick and stucco. what a pain it must be to flee from your home, to flee from bloodthirsty strangers and stand beside a pile of rubble.

Often, as we travel through the countryside, people shake their fist or give us a well-placed centre finger. At first I was a little bitter, this was not the reaction I am used to or expected. While in Kuwait I got a little tired of shaking hands and waving to the civilians. In Kuwait people understood that we were there to help and protect them. In Croatia, where no one trusts soldiers of any sort, they see us as some sort of trouble, but I will keep on doing my duty of protecting nations that wish for peace. I will risk my life daily using the special skills I have been given by my country to help keep civilians and UN soldiers safe in travel and daily function.

At the moment I am traveling from infantry checkpoint to checkpoint and teaching private soldiers and officers alike about the mines (anti-personnel and anti-tank), unexploded ordnance, and booby traps, that are still too frequent. We stress that one engineer has died, a well-trained man. As well, one Cpl infantryman who stepped outside an area that was clear lost his foot.

I feel proud as a Canadian, and proud to be part of the Canadian Engineer Corps, without a doubt the world's best trained and respected. My only regret is I am not with my regiment. I feel like an adopted son who doesn't get the love and respect the adoptive parents should give. {Brian Isfeld note: Mark's regiment at the time was stationed in Daruvar and his section was attached to the infantry. He nicknamed his section 'the lost boys2'.}

I feel compelled to say that the support of the loved ones and wives who miss us all so much is unparalleled. It takes a special person to weather the storm alone at home while their husbands are worlds away and in dangerous situations constantly. While we may laugh at being shot at or finding mines, our loved ones get sick from 6 months of constant worry. I love my wife, but I am very confident in my knowledge and ability to keep myself from danger. I understand this. How can she? She cannot understand why I would want to touch a bomb that is set to go off with very little pressure, or that may have a booby trap on it.

The only answer I can give is, I know what this stuff can do. Civilians, small children don't. My skills are to protect them. Engineers think of how many lives they are saving, not of the one they risk.

Mark

Days off and leaves were vital elements of a six-month deployment. Sometimes Mark stayed on the compound finding relaxation in the simple things. *The day is winding down, I've had a shower, shared some Kraft Dinner, chopped wood for the stove, now I have tea and country tunes and {I'm} ready to write letters. I get to sleep in tomorrow.*

At other times he booked his R&Rs and travelled to cities he had read about in *National Geographic* as a kid. He visited Vienna, which was less than 200 flight miles from camp. He spent three days in Opatija, where he said they served up the best seafood ever. On another leave he was so impressed with Budapest he called it a 'must return.' Mark snorkelled in the Mediterranean and rock hunted through Europe's rocky terrain, and he sent postcards home describing it all.

Photography continued to be a pleasurable distraction and he was accumulating quite a photo-journal from his unique vantage point. But he photographed more than landscapes. He recorded on film the explosive side of his job.

The infantry (PPCLI) checkpoints are always taking away arms and ammo, grenades and mortars. All this ends up in our MAD site. [Munitions Awaiting Disposal.] I have some footage of some BIPS we did [blow in place]. So you'll see how.

Mark joked about one day taking a Pulitzer-Prize-winning shot and whenever possible packed his camera — just in case. Making videos was more than collecting images to refer to in his later years. On one occasion he intended to film something he hoped would alleviate the stress burdening his parents and his wife. It wasn't exactly what most moms and dads would have expected. Not footage of Mark relaxing on the base petting a stray kitten the troop had adopted or of soldiers waving to Mark's family on cue — it was a video of Mark disarming an anti-personnel landmine. Calmly explaining each step, he meticulously scraped away the soft dirt from on top of the landmine, half hidden in a grassy field. His fingers disappeared under the menace, then delicately pulling the housing from the dirt he hoisted it into the air. Peering into the eye of the camera he pronounced, *It's almost as good as a fish, Dad!*

He exuded such confidence that his parents proudly referred to it over the years as proof of their son's skill. In 1994 the National Film Board would request this video clip to add to their film about 1CER.

"Nothing that grieves us can be called little: by the eternal laws of proportion, a child's loss of a doll and a king's loss of a crown are events of the same size."

Mark Twain

The villages of Croatia were quaint with their historic personalities. Mark commented how strange it was to see a row of houses intact and then one home or a targeted row selectively razed. It was a sign of ethnic cleansing, the violent and terrifying enforced removal of a people. He called it terrible and sad.

While driving through one such hamlet, Mark pulled his truck into a yard that had been chosen and destroyed. He stopped his truck and scanned the lot. A doll lay strewn atop a pile of rubble; at first glance it resembled the body of a tiny toddler face down in the debris. In the background, stood the unrecognizable wreckage of a home. Perhaps it was the house where the doll's owner had lived, and in the family's frantic escape was left behind. Mark grabbed his camera from the truck and, with the snap of the shutter, captured the pathos of the abandoned yard where not long ago children romped and played.

Children of war who are caught in an exodus rarely had possessions, and rarer still, toys to comfort them. Personal belongings were either destroyed or left behind in an evacuation situation. Mark told his wife and his mother about the photograph he had taken and said that he hoped it would turn out. For Mark it would be more than a picture, it would be a statement of the sacrifice forced upon the children of war.

He stuffed the roll of film in his bag with other rolls waiting to be developed upon his return home.

***

As strategically planned, Mark's Christmas leave in December of 1992 was approved to accommodate his and Kelly's anniversary. It was a much needed vacation to reconnect with family and friends but Mark was also eagerly anticipating getting his film developed.

Mark and Kelly stood outside the print store with the envelope of photos from the first half of Mark's tour. They scrolled through the stack and Mark stopped at the image he was looking for; the doll in the rubble. Kelly remembers how pleased Mark was that the photo he was waiting for had turned out. He made extra copies for his parents.

During their visit with his mother and father he described the details of when and where the photo was taken. Mark emphasized the reoccurring fact that children in war zones did not have a childhood. He told his mother something she reiterated in interviews in later years, "A little girl has lost her doll and a doll has lost her little girl." Her son's compassion moved her and she said she had to do something to help the children and bring peace to her son's mind.

It was good to be home for the holiday season, but Mark was agitated and unable to resume the normalcy he remembered. The disparity between the abundance and waste of the holiday season in Canada and the destitute conditions for many in war-torn regions weighed heavily on his shoulders. Although it was a dilemma he could not ignore, he did find a way to reconcile his feelings. In January he wrote a letter to his pen-pal about his Christmas holidays:

When I got home, the very next day I chose five kids from a Salvation Army tree in the mall. They have tree ornaments with names and wish lists and Kelly and I spent over two hundred US before I would spend on anyone at home. Seemed like such a frivolous waste. But over all I calmed down and got into the usual giving spirit. Good thing for the kids eh?

It was cathartic for Mark to buy gifts for the children named on the Salvation Army Christmas tree. To challenge the sense of hopelessness by a simple act of kindness gave him a measure of control. It was healing.

Remember when in a country like this, trust no one; only a few do the fighting that kills many and destroys much. And all sides feel they are right.
Mark's comments on returning to Croatia after his leave

Mark returned to snowy Camp Polom where, surprisingly, the weather was comparable to an Edmonton winter, blizzards included. He was immediately clearing mines and booby traps and he noted the high number of incidents they had had over the holiday season. He wrote that his mood was dark. Not only did he not want to return to this troubled part of the world, he was frustrated with some NCOs (Non-commissioned Officers) he described as *grown men who are supposed to set examples for the young sappers and who were acting like the south end of a donkey going north.*

To add to this, the pay for his previous Peacekeepers' tour was finally being dealt with. *Kuwait is not over - still haunting me. They decided to pay us full benefits for Kuwait so I got retroactive pay…*

But what was given was promptly taken away. Over half the cheque was 'recovered' – Mark did not understand why and, on top of that, the government charged him a $100 penalty for the recovery.

It was shocking that deployed soldiers have to fight such unnecessary battles triggered by people within their own country. At a time when his government should have been his 'pal' Mark said they were not. He showed control in setting the issue aside to remain focused on his job for safety's sake, but he intended to address the issue after the mission. *Kind of sucks and no answers. They just took it away. I'm going to be quiet about it here but when I get home I will demand answers and if I find negligence I will write Ottawa.*

∗∗∗

Mark said the fighting had erupted in their region and that they teetered on the fulcrum of peace. They were put on a four-hour notice to move, which quickly changed to a fifteen-minute notice, and then an actual change in location.

It is a little unnerving waiting to find out if you will be drawn into combat. We have been preparing to fight, and one night we moved out in a "blocking action"… It put me in a frame of mind that has not left yet. Sort of like waiting in a doctor's office for news, expecting the worst, hoping for the best. They have said they will fight us. Intelligence says they are building up strength on both sides of us. Time will tell.

It was important to Mark that he continue to deliver the facts to his family so they were not in the dark, but he also knew they needed a constant dose of reassurance.

As it stands now we have Croats on our east and west sides and they plan to take the ground we are protecting within two weeks. I guess it is up to the UN to decide what it is worth. We may have to fight or we may just pull out the UN forces… I find the job satisfying and I'm confident we are powerful and morale is very good.

Mark was aware that his parents would handle the stress of his deployment as their unique personalities dictated. He sent encouraging comments along with his trademark humour.

Be nice to each other and try to be patient and show each other if only once a day that you love each other. Don't worry about me. Although this letter may sound terrible, I am fine and I'm safe and happy. My job is good and fulfilling. I'm responsible for saving lives I'll never know. Every piece of ordnance I destroy under control saves a life.

Don't believe what you hear on the news. I heard we had all moved to Sarajevo. Well, if that's true they forgot to take me. Truly all is fine and I'm fat. I think I've gained 5 pounds of pure fat. Ha.

Your loving son M

THE DOLLS ARRIVE

A gift of small proportion, crocheted and freely shared
To cheer the grieving children. After ravages of war
To fit a soldier's pocket, who understood their toll
It won the people's smiles and hearts, this homemade Izzy Doll

Excerpt from Phyllis' Izzy Doll song

Mark peeled the brown outer wrap from the package his mother told him she was sending. He was curious to see the dolls and he lined them up, all twenty-one, side by side. Made with scraps of bright variegated yarn, each was unique and brought a smile to Mark's face as he admired his mother's handy-work. These crocheted toys were Carol's answer to his photo of the doll in the rubble. He was pleased with the little boy dolls with blue berets and the little girls with pigtails. But most of all, said Brian, Mark was relieved that his mom had found a hands-on project to deflect some of her worry.

Just as his mother had hoped, Mark carried a doll in his uniform pocket. Whenever he met a child he gave the gift of a doll and watched what happened next. First the child's eyes lit up, then a smile formed. As they exchanged friendly grins their mistrust for this Peacekeeper disappeared.

Mark talked about how good it felt to offer a gift of hope in a climate of uncertainty. He photographed members of his troop experiencing the feeling of goodwill as they gave out dolls, too. Mark became known as the Peacekeeper who, as his section commander Sgt Greg James put it, collected little hearts, little smiles and little handshakes.

There is no doubt the Serb Major would like nothing more than to see us leave, as we are in control, and keep proving him a liar!! We also keep all his weapons!!

Mark's comment about a Serbian officer

Peacekeepers continued to confiscate and destroy stashes of ammunition belonging to the warring factions. Irritated by the actions of the UNPROFOR soldiers, the enemy forces used trickery and deceit to discredit the Peacekeepers.

Seriously I am in an embittered mood of late, having been part of the Serbian farce. Being privy to a conversation that went on between my troop warrant officer and Major Tiger, the Serbian officer, regarding the hostile way we hold our weapons toward little children, and how we take the food out of their mouths by driving through the fields. As well we drive our trucks on their roads and leave them in a muddy state as an insult to them. We were also made into propaganda pictures in all these cases because the Serb Major posed little kids near us, and old ladies.

The proliferation and endorsement of hatred being handed down angered Mark to the core, but it was the locals who restored his commitment. *Although I was angry and felt like just leaving these people to their own devices, I remembered that he is the evil sort who caused all the problems here, and on our way back to Polom people came to the road side to wave at the "blue hats", and I threw candy to the little kids. Who, I might add, are far from spoiled and share. I wonder how long it takes to teach them the war mentality their elders thrive on? Yes, I certainly do look forward to our own lovely kind of chaos in Canada.*

All my love, your peacekeeper M.

Confrontations with Serb and Croat forces were frequent and, in Mark's words, it was a feeling of tension that could snap easily. He said that each encounter he had experienced was carefully diffused by the Peacekeepers. After one particular resolution, one of the Serb soldiers shook Mark's hand showing regret about their confrontation. Mark interpreted this as a sign that other soldiers were in the mood for peace too.

***

Mark continued to do well on his personal evaluation reports, coming in fifth out of ninety corporals. He consistently showed a high regard for his job and the men and women of the 1CER, but compounding stresses were strong enough to force him to consider a career change. The deciding factor came when Kelly's father had a heart attack during Mark's deployment and he felt frustrated that he couldn't be there for his wife. As a result he submitted a formal request to re-muster as a welder in the air force and wrote to his parents saying, *I'm happy as an engineer; I will always admire them and be one of them, but I'm prepared to move on to something new. The good times don't outweigh the hard any more.* A career move was a proactive strategy to lessen the strain on himself and his family. However, the job request never materialized.

✳✳✳

In April 1993 Mark had completed his second tour of duty. He came home and tried to resume a normal life, but his tours of duty had affected the way he saw the world – literally.

Leigh said that his brother had difficulty adjusting. Mark had described the vivid colours of the flowers in his much-loved garden as dull. Their vibrancy was dimmed. He also told his brother that he trusted that, with time, the colours of his world would return.

There were additional concerns for a soldier between tours of duty. Mark's third tour, second in the former Yugoslavia, was approaching and now Mark held another role that needed his attention — family man.

Mark wrote that he tried to anticipate what repairs and upgrades should be made to the house so Kelly wasn't overwhelmed while he was away. He was well aware that a military wife didn't need the added pressure.

✳✳✳

Prior to leaving on his third tour, Mark talked frankly to his dad. Brian wrote about their conversation:

"Mark had experienced many of the realities of damage a war does to people and countries, and just before leaving on this trip told me: 'Dad, I don't feel good about this trip. Something is going to happen. Not necessarily to me but I don't like it.' {It was} Completely out of character for Mark and it troubled me. Not a great deal, but there was still the chance he could be right. His approach this time was one of pure professionalism. He wanted to get over there, do his job, and get home. No excitement. No ebullience. Just apprehension. He had told me that he was resigned to the fact that the situation in Croatia was not going to change in the near future and that he could see no end in sight. He said it had the makings of another Cyprus for the Canadians, and he expected to see much more of Croatia before anything was resolved."

THIRD UN PEACEKEEPING MISSION CROATIA

I have made some good friends on both sides, but one particularly good friend, Filip, a Croatian Lt. infantry soldier. Together we became friends in a way that is hard to explain. He knows, I know, and no one else can. We cleared a field of six anti personnel mines in waist high grass with trip wires all around. When we had it cleared we shook hands as if the unspoken words were understood... He is truly in the mood for peace.

Mark, April 27, 1994

Shortly after arriving in the former Yugoslavia in April 1994, Mark wrote home with his trademark optimism. He told his family that he was encouraged with the breadth of his duties and he believed he was making a difference.

I have been doing a lot of mine lift supervision or overseeing, recording data, negotiating, communicating concerns and encouraging the lifting of mines and minefields that are not necessarily on our patrol routes, in the hopes of saving lives of soldiers, civilians and animals. Peacekeeping, in the true sense, like I have never been so directly exposed to previously.

Everything is fine with us. No need to worry, your son is fine and I think making a difference in this part of the world. All my love I'll write again soon.

M.

Some of the more rewarding work came when liaising with both sides. 1CER supervised mine lifting with both Serb and Croat soldiers (who were responsible for the seeding of the mines in the first place). According to Mark they were successful, covering a lot of ground and lifting approximately 600 both anti-personnel and anti-tank mines within five weeks.

A Croatian light-infantry soldier named Filip won Mark's respect for his willingness to help clear the land and also for divulging information that led to additional landmines being found.

Filip is without a doubt my most reliable ally in this operation. He looks at mine records and takes me aside and secretly gives me numbers, types and locations. I then work on him to "come lift with us." He is very concerned about my welfare and is constantly looking out for me telling me "Mark in this area you go slow."

During Filip's three years in this war, Mark said he had only seen his family twice. Mark gave his new friend a Canadian flag and one of his mother's dolls for Filip's three-year-old daughter. Making partnerships like this was a hopeful sign and once again proof that soldiers on each side wanted peace.

***

Packages of dolls continued to arrive from Canada and Mark continued to lift the spirits of the little ones. In a letter to his maternal grandparents Mark wrote about the children's reactions. *I've seen some big smiles... One little girl was thrilled with the pony tails.*

His tours of duty were stressful and ugly, but also hopeful. As a soldier Mark straddled two worlds. For him, growing up in Canada and deeply entrenched in the principles of equality and fundamental human rights, peace was more than a concept; it was real. Mark did not abandon his principles, freely giving dolls without prejudice. General Lewis MacKenzie noted that Mark saw neither Serb, Muslim, nor Croat; he only saw a child.

There has been a mine accident which you are already aware of in which an Iltis (jeep) ran over a mine [and a young canadian infantryman lost both legs and an eye] in our area. Enough about that.

Excerpt from Mark's letter, April 27, 1994

The bloody clashing of wills, landmine accidents rendering soldiers or civilians crippled or dead, and the exodus of fleeing villagers, was described by one Canadian soldier as absurd and ridiculous. The horrific acts of war were so incongruent with anything these Canadian men and women deployed here had ever experienced, it was certain to raise their stress levels.

To cope with the stress, the Canadian soldiers did what soldiers have been doing for centuries; they organized competitive sports and contests that challenged their strength and skill. Physical exertion has been known to help people focus and relax, relieving some of the emotional and mental burdens. And every once in a while, the flag of humour was raised that paralleled the absurdity around them. In May, Mark wrote:

We are having a bit of a war with the other engineers who are located across the street from us. They put up a sign so we had to outdo them. We are in the bad books with the transport officer at CANLOGBAT. We painted a Klingon (Star Trek) symbol on any vehicle that comes into our compound and they don't like it. We almost got a helicopter, but someone stopped the culprit.

***

In early May the PAFFO, or Public Affairs Office, National Defence, visited with guests from the National Film Board. Mark and his section were interviewed and videotaped for a documentary on 1CER and their duties as Sappers. Mark's experience with his camera paid off; he was supplied with a quality camera and asked to take footage of mine clearing whenever possible. He commented that he would like to buy a camera just like this one someday, perhaps even become a photojournalist.

Garth Pritchard, the director, shot dramatic close-ups of Mark and his troop clearing mines with expert precision. Just weeks after filming, a tragic and shocking turn of events established the documentary's new ending, which literally epitomized the title of the film, *Price of Duty.*

YOU'VE LOST A GOOD ONE, CANADA

"Intensely serious about his job, he had studied every piece of known ordnance in Croatia, could recognize it from 100 paces away, and take it apart blindfolded. He was supremely confident in his skills; not cocky, but purely professional. How cruelly ironic that his finely honed skills were irrelevant in the way he died. He happened to be outside an armoured personnel carrier when it ran over the trip wire to an anti-personnel mine. Wrong place, wrong time."

An excerpt from Andy Holota's article in the Surrey Leader

M̲ark was counting down the days when he would board the plane for his next leave. It wasn't an exotic location but it was his favourite destination. Home.

Mark's father outlined the details of what happened June 21, 1994, as they were told to him.

"The section, consisting of Sappers Merriam, Taillefeur, Corporal Klassen, Sgt {Greg} James, infantry Sgt Paul Macmillan and of course Mark, had cleared an area along a dike to gain access to a water pipe which the Serbs or Croats, or possibly the Chetniks, had blown up previously.

"As Mark was guiding an armoured personnel carrier up the side of a berm, and Greg and Sgt Macmillan were standing about 30 metres away on a cement abutment, the carrier apparently set off a mine in the tall (one metre or more) grass. This in turn set off a mine in the close proximity to Mark, killing him and injuring the other two, Greg and Paul. The mine was one designated PROM-1, an insidious contraption, designed to be buried in the ground, and when set off bounds up a distance of about 1 metre, exploding. It has about 500-700 steel balls inside it, 5 mm in diameter. Upon reaching 1 metre above the ground it explodes, due to a wire attached to the base, which stays in the ground. The ensuing explosion directs the balls and fragments of the mine in a 360 degree area.

"Mark was hit from a distance of about three metres, at abdomen level, and was severely wounded from the waist down … In the words of the official death certificate, 'Heavy hemorrhagenic shock.'

"Greg and Paul were knocked off the cement pads and were down in the tall grass, which had started to burn, being ignited by the blast. Sappers Merriam and Taillefeur came over top the carrier from the rear, and immediately went to Mark where Merriam, or 'Hollywood' as he is known to the troops, began to give CPR to Mark. He stuffed a combat shirt into the largest wound and at the same time gave Mark mouth to mouth resuscitation. He gained and lost a pulse three times in the process, with Mark not responding in any other way. In the

38

meantime 'Tally', sizing up the situation and realizing that Greg and Paul could be burned to death in the field, went to their aid, and with the aid of the medics from the ambulance, which is always near by on an operation like this, pulled the two of them to safety. A helicopter was dispatched and arrived in about 14 minutes which was very good time, and took Mark and Greg to Knin, Croatia, where there is a Czech field hospital. They lost and regained Mark's pulse in the helicopter two or three times. He died officially on the operating table in Knin, but for me, I will always believe that he died at the moment of the explosion, and only the efforts of the individuals involved and their overwhelming desire to save one of their brothers kept the pulse and adrenaline flowing. I shall always be grateful to Tally and Hollywood for their efforts and they have a place in my heart and home evermore."

Brian made note of additional comments from one of the soldiers: "Brian, Mark was not out that day lifting mines for peace, or for the kids or civvies, or for Canada or the United Nations. Operation Trident was one of the most important tasks we had to date. He was killed attempting to make the ground safe so his 'Buddies' in the infantry could get on with the job they had to do without the fear of getting their nuts blown off. We loved him."

Mark was laid to rest in Little Mountain Royal Canadian Legion Cemetery, Chilliwack, British Columbia, Canada, on June 27, 1994. Red roses, long stemmed symbols of love, were draped over his casket one by one, by his wife and family. Kelly and the Isfelds felt an outpouring of generosity and support. It was an indicator of a larger community who grieved, too, affected by the loss of their friend and a fellow Canadian who could never be replaced. Brian wrote, "And so ends the letters and life of one peacekeeper. One who had the promise of an excellent career ahead of him. One who had the promise of a

very happy life with his beloved wife. One who can be seen from his letters to have been tough yet gentle, brave yet careful, boisterous yet conscientious. A loving, caring, hard working loyal soldier; loved and cared for deeply by many."

"None die, in the memory of those who live."
Author unknown

Immediately after Mark's death, Carol and Brian made a resolution that their son would be one soldier who would not be forgotten. A series of memorial projects in Mark's name led curious Canadians to ask "Who was this soldier?" With every question, Mark's spirit was and is revived, living on, just as his parents had intended.

For thirteen years the Isfelds were enthusiastic stewards of the Izzy Doll project and carried the torch to ban landmines. They had remained deeply committed but it was not an easy road. Some people described Carol and Brian as ordinary people who accomplished extraordinary deeds. Others say there is plenty of proof that the divine hand of something or someone had interceded at critical crossroads to help them along the way.

THE BROTHERHOOD

"I now know why men who have been to war yearn to reunite. Not to tell stories or look at old pictures. Not to laugh or weep. Comrades gather because they long to be with the men who once acted at their best; men who suffered and sacrificed, who were stripped of their humanity. I did not pick these men. They were delivered by fate and the military. But I know them in a way I know no other men. I have never given anyone such trust. They were willing to guard something more precious than my life. They would have carried my reputation, the memory of me. It was part of the bargain we all made, the reason we were so willing to die for one another. As long as I have my memory, I will think of them all, every day. I am sure that when I leave this world, my last thought will be of my family and my comrades ... such good men."

Author unknown

More than an investment in each other's security, the brotherhood of soldiers is a relationship forged under the intense pressure of living and working together under the most demanding conditions. Both male and female soldiers share the common denominator of enduring the worst while giving their best, and it results in a lasting bond that is diamond-like — rare and beautiful.

It has been explained to me that the Brotherhood of soldiers can be as close as a birth family, with relationships as strong as connections with siblings.

Nicknames can reflect the camaraderie of a brotherhood and Mark was widely known as Izzy, an abbreviation of his last name, given to him by his buddies. When the fatal landmine explosion injured two of their own and killed Izzy, the Brotherhood reacted as though they had lost a family member.

Padre Captain John Organ was the attending Padre on the front lines of the emotional fallout. He brought the engineers together in an intimate circle and facilitated the release of grief and tears as each soldier talked about the events that led to the deadly accident. As well, a memorial service on the base was held for military personnel.

Everyone grieves in his or her own way and these hands-on soldiers, action oriented and accustomed to finding solutions, created their own unique tribute. As engineers do, they executed a plan for a memorial befitting their brother's Icelandic heritage. In the confines of their compound, they constructed a display of honour — a replica Viking ship complete with a sail, oars, shields, and a dragon-like figurehead. In a symbolic gesture for a revered fellow warrior, they then ceremoniously torched the ship. It burned in fiery splendour against the night, sending Mark's spirit to Odin's Table in the mythical Valhalla, where the fallen are gathered.

Padre Organ contacted Carol and Brian explaining the details of the circumstances of Mark's death. He also shone a light on the actions of 1CER. Of this occasion he wrote:

The Engineer Troop held the Viking custom of burning a boat to commemorate a friend's passing and to symbolize this spirit's ascending from the earth. It was an emotional and wonderfully moving ceremony. Watching the sparks from the fire ascend into the night sky and seemingly blend into the stars of heaven, it was as if Mark's spirit was leaving the bonds of earth and being set free to know the wonder, mystery and glory of all that is holy and good in the universe. He was going from us and that was painful, but he was ascending to that place where everything is right, whole and pure.

Weeks later Mark's family and friends gathered together for his funeral held in Chilliwack. After the gravesite service, grief stricken, they slowly withdrew.

However, his second family remained. The Brotherhood — seven striking figures representing the 1CER stood in solemn repose, instinctively poised to perform a final act of respect and honour. Knowing it would bring some solace to Brian and Carol, one of the seven wrote to tell of their last hours and final good-byes with Mark.

… I must tell you this story and I hope you don't mind. When the funeral service at the gravesite had ended and all the people had gone, there were seven engineers remaining. We all stood around Mark and just couldn't pull ourselves away. It seemed like an eternity, but our memories of Mark were interrupted when a tractor and two caretakers came over the hill. We turned and stared at the machine and then back at each other.

Strangely, we all had the same thoughts at the same time. When the tractor pulled up, we approached and asked if we could lower Mark. They agreed and we each took turns lowering him. When that was done, again we all looked at each other quietly, and still not wanting to leave asked the caretakers if they had any shovels. They did. We all removed our tunics, rolled up our sleeves and did what we felt was the honourable thing for Mark, Kelly and the children, you, Kelly's mom and dad, his brothers, friends and relatives and that motley group of soldiers who never say no and never know when to quit, the Canadian Combat Engineers.

He meant so much to so many people and we could not stand by and let strangers lay Mark to rest… The engineers hold you very near and dear to our hearts. Just as we did Mark…

Your friend always,
John Payne

Brian Isfeld made a note of the seven soldiers who were there that day. They were Warrant officer Dan Hartford, Sergeant (now Warrant Officer) John Payne, Sergeant Joe Thomas, Sergeant J Love (air force), Master Corporal "Teddy" Tedesco, Corporal Harry Eegeesiak, Corporal Rob Cayley

1CER had one more deed to complete. They were witness to Izzy's beaming smile while packing homemade knitted dolls in his uniform pockets — they even teased him about it in the beginning. But as they, too, began to give out dolls they could attest to the joy of the children, hands outstretched to receive these gifts. It was a good feeling, a momentary pleasure that indeed lifted the spirits of the giver and receiver even in the midst of the most forsaken circumstances. It was at this point that Mark's troop named the dolls the Izzy Dolls after their friend and brother.

In a third act of love 1CER made a deal with Carol Isfeld. Because they could not allow the distribution of Izzy's dolls to stop they said to Mark's mother; "If you continue to make the dolls, we would like to continue to give them to the children."

Carol said she was overjoyed at 1CER's benevolence that would ensure the children of war were not forgotten, and that her son would be remembered through this legacy project.

It was at this moment that the Izzy Doll began to take on its stature as a phenomenon - not yet in numbers, but in its direction. No longer a mother and son project, the 1CER had given the Izzy Doll wings — wings that would take this homemade toy to the farthest reaches of the earth, cheering hundreds of thousands of children in the years to come.

Carol said she was forever grateful and embraced the Brotherhood of Engineers as her sons and daughters. She penned this poem just for them:

"An Engineer's Prayer" My Prayer for you all

May you always travel at God's speed, safe and sure,
May your steps only come when the road is made secure.

May you always know in your heart, your Brothers are there.
They are an extension of you, your space they share.

May your sleep at night be restful, and sound,
May the next step you take be on safe ground.

May you always know, unconditionally,
With your last thought at night;
Remember, we at home love you,
Though you're not in our sight.

Love, Mom

Carol Isfeld, Nov 1994

CHAPTER 2

CAROL ISFELD
JUNE 2, 1939 – AUGUST 15, 2007

Carol and Kelly

THE LITTLE GIRL WITH THE BIG HEART

"children are the 'well' the future will draw on. In them is the strength, energy, power, passions, courage, generosity and farsightedness. shelter, love and care for them today, teach them well and truthfully. They hold the world in their hands"

From Carol Isfeld's Book "My Poems"

Motherhood is not for the starry eyed. It is true there are moments when a mom might briefly catch herself in awe of the infant in her arms and of the unbelievable miracle of it all. There is joy. But the degree of commitment to this tiny human being, so dependent, so helpless, drains any rebel euphoria that might seek to gush. Then add fear.

Motherhood fluctuates between a range of emotions, with two more predominant than others; fear and hope. There is a mother's hope of seeing her babies grow into productive adults, loving what they choose to do, and giving back to the world that rents them the air and space to grow until the end of a long and full life. Paralleling hope, and with every step of the way, is the fear that her hopes will not materialize. Carol Isfeld knew this roller coaster ride all too well.

Born in 1939 in Winnipeg and raised in the picturesque village of Brownsburg at the foot of Quebec's Laurentian Mountains, Carol Donaldson was the eldest of five children born to Olina and George Elmer Donaldson. Brownsburg was like any other Canadian community recovering from the dirty thirties and the great economic depression. The Donaldsons struggled to make do with what they had and consequently everything was homemade, from meals prepared from scratch, to hand-crafted gifts for birthdays and Christmas. Mr. Donaldson had 'the artist touch' and would design and sew Halloween costumes for his children that often won first place at school.

The Donaldsons shared their garden produce with neighbours and lent a hand when someone was in need. Making do with what they had was a way of life, and helping each other was a condition for survival.

An inquisitive little girl, Carol had an engaging smile and compassionate heart. As a ten year-old she had already begun discerning the needs of others outside of her family. Mr. Turner, the town garbage collector, was a well-known public figure. On one particular wintry morning when his horse and sleigh pulled into the Donaldson driveway, there was a surprise helper all ready to go with him. Carol stood waiting, all bundled up in winter jacket, toque, and mitts. She reasoned he surely needed her help and eagerly offered to be his assistant. She climbed aboard and they disappeared down the street. It didn't take long for her parents to realize that she was missing. They scoured the town, frantic that their daughter was in harm's way.

Garbage pickup completed, Carol arrived home pleased as pie and greeted by two frantic parents. She was just being herself after all, and finding ways to help and serve others became the template for her future.

Family life as the eldest daughter prepared her for motherhood. She would pass on the wise mantras that had been passed down to her: Make do with what you have, and if someone is in need, help.

Carol grew into womanhood with a trademark smile that few could forget, particularly Brian Isfeld. Young Brian looked sharp in his RCAF uniform and caught Carol's eye, too. They fell in love and married. After the birth of their first son, Leigh, they were stationed in Germany, where their two younger sons Mark and Glenn were born. Carol's roots ran deep and she was homesick for her family back in Canada. She missed Brian's family, too, whom she considered more than in-laws. Her only sister, Judy MacGibbon, reflected: "Carol loved coming home to visit Mom & Dad. After their stint in Germany she hardly missed a year. It was a necessity in her life to touch roots constantly. Carol also considered Brian's only sibling Pat (McKenzie) one of her best friends and her other sister."

Judy smiles as she talks of Carol's fashion sense and how easily she could create a stylish outfit, mixing and matching colours and patterns. Judy added, "Carol's biggest attribute was her generosity of heart. She was known for her one-liners, too, a very quick mind. She loved her car, reading, and oh yes, her Bingo."

The Donaldson children had inherited their father's artistic gene and several became artists themselves. For Carol, art was an outlet for her emotions. Pragmatic and creative, she would surrender to her intuitive instincts reinventing or adapting a ceramic mould to personalize a special gift. She painted floral scenes and wildlife onto canvas and she wrote poetry to express whatever she could not say with brushes or paint.

Carol was known for her poetry, which she loved to compose. As an idea or thought moved her she would scribble it on scraps of paper or serviettes; whatever was handy. Later she copied them into her floral-covered book that friends Dave and Lynn Breese had given her. With a silver marker she had personalized it with the title *My Poems* along its dark blue binding. But the content was far more than poetry.

As I turned the pages of the book, I sensed this was a vault where she stored her deepest emotions; a safe place where she could shout out her anger and disappointments in private. She wrote stanzas that reflected her thoughts on love and duty: *Love is an emotion, God is love* and *Two of the saddest words are 'If only'. The four best ones are 'I'm glad I did.'* Carol used rhyming words to create poems for birthdays and special occasions. She confided to her friends that creating poems was like therapy — something she just had to do. Over decades, the tumultuous highs and lows of her life that had morphed into poetry became a recorded history of Carol's past.

> *"While we try to teach our children all about life, our children teach us what life is all about."*
> Angela Schwindt, homeschooling mom from Oregon, U.S.

Carol was born a humanitarian, motivated by an innate desire to bring comfort and peace of mind to others. The sight of a hurting animal, a child in need, or issues that affected the aged and vulnerable was always a concern. Leigh described his mom as everybody's grandmother. "She was always thinking of others first, ate last. She was a humanitarian serving people all her life. Mom was the kind of person who gave emotional support and direction. She encouraged the spirit in us. She might not be able to put a model plane together but she knew how to make you feel so you believed you could do it yourself."

At certain points during the raising of my own children, I experienced Ah-ha moments as I realized the tremendous work and the sacrifices my parents made raising me and my seven siblings. I have no doubt that most parents come to this awareness too. Carol had her Ah-ha moments while her three sons were going through their adolescence — at the same time. She wrote Masters of All Trades which is filled with praise and deep respect for her mother and father, and for the many roles they had played in her life.

Masters of all Trades - My Parents Olina and George Elmer Donaldson

They were artists: *Dad painted pictures of beautiful things everywhere. With words, mom painted pictures of love and patience — All for me.*

They were electricians: *They kept me plugged into the present with lessons that connected me to my future — They wired me.*

They were Doctors: *Mended cuts, bruises, bumps, broken dolls, dreams and broken hearts — Then they kissed me.*

They were ministers: *They watched and listened to my life, taught me about God, faith and love, hope, charity forgiveness and feelings — And they loved me.*

They were builders and teachers: *I learned to cook, mend and clean. They could make or fix anything. They built my home on a rock. They even helped Santa and the tooth fairy — They kept teaching me.*

They were Police: *They kept curfew, made sure I knew right from wrong. Taught me we have to pay for mistakes big or small, examples were given — They showed me.*

Babysitters: *They were always there — They never left me.*

They were the Postal service, telephone operators: *They never forgot me, no matter how far, remembered special dates, special New Year's call. And they just called to talk. They are connected to me — They are me and I love them so.*

Carol and Brian were overjoyed when Leigh and his wife Judy made them grandparents, twice. They chose to name their sons Brian and Mark in honour of Grandpa Brian and Uncle Mark. Carol wrote about the 'special powers' of a grandchild in her poem To Be a Grandma:

Those little eyes gazed into mine
Babies do have special powers
Tiny, perfect works of art
Soft as petals on a flower
I looked into that tiny face

Something happened deep inside
I didn't really dare to breathe
My heart swelled so with pride

I ached I felt so happy
Tears came, and years receded
To hug and hold a baby now
Was exactly what I needed

I saw again, my son, his father,
I felt the same, so long ago
I'm sure it's how my own mom felt
Now I know what grandmas know

For a mother, it is a blessing when your child understands and 'gets' who you are. Mark was aware of his mom's apprehension for his chosen field, and he also understood that poetry was her favourite means of expression. So just before leaving on his second tour of duty in 1992, he asked her to write down her thoughts about war. Appropriately she called the piece Thoughts on War.

Our lives are in a turmoil, But then so is Man.
There's been some sort of conflict, Ever since the world began.
There's so much hate and greed and jealousy. God! Help each one of us to care.
We forgot you gave us love and trust, So call your neighbour friend — and share.

Only weeks later, she wrote a poem for Mark's birthday called *My Son, Our Sons*. Carol dedicated it to "Peacekeepers from all walks of life, from all nations and to the mothers of these Peacekeepers who carry on regardless." It was later adapted as a song by composer Jan Randall, from Edmonton Alberta, and added to Mark's memorial website as the background music:

You are going away my son,
For reasons only God can understand.
We're told you're trying to keep the peace
With our hurting fellow man.

I know that each of our sons
Will make a friend with someone there.
They are taking love from home
It will show them how we care.

They have been warring for decades
Now they're killing each other.
Where does all the hate begin
To make us want to kill a brother?

I see my son leaving soon
For a hopeless situation.
That's my understanding
For this very troubled nation.

I love you. Mom

Carol M. Isfeld, 14 August 1992

Carol at the opening of Peacekeeper Park in Calgary, Alberta

THE BIRTH OF THE IZZY DOLL

"She is one with all women who have come before her, generations of mothers who worked their needles and crochet hooks to clothe their families. She had been taught the century-old techniques that had been passed down like a magic formula for contentment and she expresses her love through her gifts of wool and toys of yarn."

An anonymous mother and knitter about the knitter

Carol saw images within the paragraphs of Mark's letters. She saw how the very young and the very old were innocent victims in the madness of war — children begging for food and water, landmine victims with missing limbs, and the elderly abandoned and left to fend for themselves. Carol lamented the suffering and the toll she knew it would take on her son. "We talked about how things hurt us — to see others in pain and have no control over it." She knew that the constant stress was affecting him and it was certainly the reason for his sleepless nights.

The Isfelds were grateful to their son for his dedication in keeping them informed. Marks' video and photographs revealed stunning imagery as well as the ugly realities of the soldiers' surroundings. One particular photograph that spoke louder than words showed a doll lying in a heap of rubble next to what had presumably been a family home in ruin. This portrait of destruction affected Carol deeply. She was moved by Mark's empathy for the children who he said had been robbed of their childhood. She thought there must be something she could do, so, true to her nature, Carol set to work doing what she could with what she had. Turning to her knitting basket she decided to design dolls for the children of war. She could envision Mark meeting a child on his daily rounds and handing out a little doll. She could imagine their big smile that would automatically trigger a smile on Mark's face. Carol was sure that these dolls would be a worthwhile project and a positive investment of her time.

It was also a very personal and solitary mission. She sat for hours in her living room, her fluffy white puppy, Mikey, nestled in beside her on the sofa watching while she worked the stitches, testing and retrying. Her crochet hook weaved in and out transforming variegated yarn scraps into the first miniature prototype. She explained that her objective was simple; the doll had to be small enough to fit in her son's uniform pocket, be soft and safe for a child, and be easy to knit so many could be made.

Judy said of her sister, "She saw a need and filled it as she always did. Well, Carol being Carol set right to work fooling around with her yarn to create her little doll, small enough to hold in the hand of a small child and small enough for Mark to fit in his uniform pocket."

She wanted the doll to be perfect, and she knew the moment it happened. The results of her labour were pretty pastel coloured girl dolls with braids and little boy dolls who wore blue hats, just like Mark's peacekeeper beret. Carol wrapped the first package and sent it to Mark. It contained twenty-one dolls, ten of each gender and one extra. She said she didn't know why she chose those numbers but that was the size of package that she regularly sent. As she expected, Mark loved the dolls and he did just as she had hoped — carried them in his pocket and gave them out to children he met in trade for smiles and hugs. He talked about how good it felt to see the children delight in receiving a doll and how the cuddly little figures seemed to calm their fears. He told his mother that at the end of a demanding day, remembering those smiling faces actually helped him sleep.

Carol said there were other unexpected benefits too. During Mark's tour in Croatia the locals, who had a deep mistrust of any soldier, seemed genuinely thankful when their children received dolls from the Peacekeepers. There was a temporary mood shift and some parents who appreciated the generosity of the Peacekeepers actually disclosed secret locations of landmines and explosives. Carol and Brian suggested that these parents may have interpreted the dolls as gifts of goodwill and offered their disclosures as their peace offerings.

In June 1994, on Carol's birthday, Mark called home. It would be their last conversation and she remembers his emphatic request, "The dolls are a hit, Mom. Please keep making them." If the kids were happy and Mark was happy, then Carol was happy too. Mother and son had given each other something simple but great. Making the dolls gave Carol an outlet to relieve her anxiety about Mark, distributing them alleviated Mark's sense of helplessness. It was a good plan.

THE DAWN OF DREAD

"The world is incomprehensible. We won't ever understand it; we won't ever unravel its secrets. Thus we must treat the world as it is: a sheer mystery."

Carlos Castaneda

Carol's psychic gifts were a novelty — a curiosity that piqued the interest of her friends. But she also admitted that when they were painful portholes foreboding a disaster, she had a hard time considering them gifts.

A sudden and unexpected death can paralyze people, suspending them in disbelief. But for Carol, with the gift of premonition, it was a case of knowing something ominous was going to happen and waiting for the proverbial shoe to drop. She was familiar with the advent of a dream or a feeling but could usually redirect her focus until it either came true or it didn't. This time it was different.

Everyone had been thrilled to be together at Mark and Kelly's home for Christmas 1993, but for Carol this special occasion was the onset of a foreboding that would not let go.

Returning home to Courtney after the celebrations she sank into despair. She recognized the tell-tale feelings of a premonition that something catastrophic was going to happen, and there was no way she could circumvent the unknown or prepare for it. She wrote in her journal, "I was so sure something was wrong. At Mark and Kelly's house a depression deeper than ever set in after that Christmas visit... I worried so much — a sick feeling in the pit of my stomach just wouldn't go away. I literally spent six months on my knees and knowing. I wrote this poem after I got home that year:

Help
I'm in the middle of the forest, And I'm lost amongst the trees
Yet I know that God can find me, Hurt has brought me to my knees

The world is like these branches, Reaching up to feel the sun
Lord I offer you my life today, I know I'm not the only one

We know that once upon a time, One lamb got out of sight
And still today you'll find us, In our deepest, darkest night

In the spring of 1994, Mark left on his third tour. His letters and phone calls home sustained Carol's hope. Every word and every conversation meant another day closer to his returning to safe turf. When Mark called her on her birthday she listened intently to his voice. The phone call left her with a memory of a conversation that was both exciting and ominous. Happily he reported the dolls were a hit and asked her to keep sending them.

He continued the conversation with, "I'm safe… they will call Kelly first." Carol understood his reference to military protocol in the event of an accident. Should anything happen to him his next of kin would be notified, beginning with his wife. Brian had said Mark had a premonition that something was going to happen, too, but with only weeks left before Mark's scheduled return to Canada, Carol hoped that both their premonitions were wrong.

"Grief is the price we pay for love."

Queen Elizabeth II

In the early morning hours of June 21, trepidation took hold. Six months had passed since the initial forebodings began and slumber eluded her. She knew from her emotional state that a portentous event was about to reveal itself and later told friends that the dawn of day had found her on her knees fervently scrubbing her kitchen floor. She was trying to keep busy while she waited. Military officials arrived at her front door before noon and Carol's intuitions and a mother's worst fears were confirmed. Mark had been killed.

Carol's anguish spilled through the six-month-old dike, now cracked wide open. She struggled between moments of disbelief and the grim reality of it all. Friends stayed by her side until her husband's return from a family visit with his sister Pat.

Within days Judy flew out from Montreal; Brian met her at the airport. Judy acknowledges that Brian had never given credence to her sister's psychic perceptions, but during the drive from the airport he confessed, "I will never again doubt Carol's premonitions."

When a loved one dies there are details and duties that must be dealt with. Carol and Brian had additional concerns. Brian's father's health was failing, and they knew it was only a matter of days or weeks before Arilius' passing. They were also scheduled to meet with an NFB crew who were wrapping up *The Price of Duty,* a documentary featuring 1CER. Mark's unexpected death had now given the film a sombre twist.

Brian told me he didn't remember much of the interview but that he was proud of his wife for being stronger than he had felt that day. Carol was driven, perhaps because she felt the media had not given Mark's death the attention she believed it deserved. Carol had long felt that the media relegated news of soldiers' deaths to a back burner. These soldiers were real people with loved ones and lives that should be acknowledged, and she felt Canadians wanted to know more than just their names.

The cameras rolled and the NFB crew recorded a distraught mother speaking her mind, exasperated at the lack of media attention given to the deaths of Canadian soldiers… and now her son's. "Each and every time our men have gone overseas on these peacekeeping tours it's like an afterthought to show them getting on a plane or off a plane … and then they're showing some murder or some bloody thing about the taxes … each man that gets murdered or hurt over there — it's the third or fourth thing on the news and I always got upset because I wanted to see the person and feel for them, but this time it was my son and I had to listen to OJ Simpson bullshit and some American soldier gunning down a bunch of people … and then there's an afterthought — by the way there's one more Canadian soldier died."

The Isfelds' fear that their son's death might be dismissed as an afterthought was foremost in their minds and it bolstered their conviction that "This would be one soldier who would not be forgotten."

***

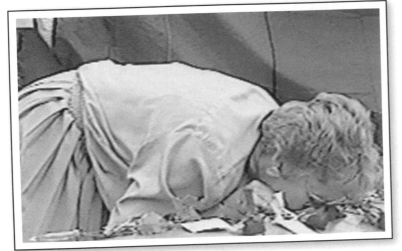

If there was a ray of sunshine during the days surrounding Mark's funeral it was an offer Carol couldn't refuse that was generated by the engineers and brothers of 1CER. She described their request to continue distributing the dolls they had nicknamed Izzy Dolls as a wonderful surprise. Her answer was, "How could I not?" Their words wrapped around her like warm hugs affirming what Mark had started with the dolls was worthy and important to them, too.

Carol said that when soldiers were carrying Izzy Dolls, they were 'armed' with love and goodwill; she wanted to give Mark's 'brothers' the chance to feel the same comfort Mark had felt when he collected smiles and handshakes from the children as he distributed the dolls. She gave each soldier in Mark's troop their own Izzy Doll from Mark's trunk. Coincidentally, she recalled, there just happened to be enough dolls for each of his Sapper buddies as though a personal parting gift from Mark.

There are things that we don't want to happen but have to accept, things we don't want to know but have to learn, and people we can't live without but have to let go.

Author Unknown

In the nineteen-sixties Dr. Elizabeth Kubler Ross wrote about the five stages of grief: denial, anger, bargaining, depression, and acceptance. She believed that understanding the course grief followed could help explain our own behaviour and indeed make us more sensitive to the needs of others during their losses. Each of us moves through these stages in his or her own time, for some it is brief, for others it can be agonizing and lengthy. Brian's method of grieving was to analyze the facts and the military reports trying to make sense of his son's death, and to identify any flaws that could be fixed that could save future injury or death. He set up an online memorial website for Mark and hand crafted trophies to be given in his son's honour. Carol, on the other hand, didn't want to go on. Her poetry remained filled with longing and pain.

"He" Said
"Ours is not to wonder why"
It felt no better to repeat
Why do the good ones have to die
Leaving all that's evil at our feet?

I trusted God to keep him safe
Now I'm angry and in pain
I wish I had been consulted
I have lost control again!

I know we should not question Him
He knows what's best for you
But I am left to wonder why?
And I don't know what to do.

I feel that I am losing ground
Just a mother and a wife.
The candles out – that was my guide
I'm no longer living – It's just life
I'm so lost God don't forsake me

June 21, 1996

Although she did regain her belief in God, her sister Judy explained that temporarily her faith wavered. Acceptance of Mark's death was a difficult journey and she added, "Carol grieved a long time and people told her repeatedly it had gone on too long. Boy did that make her mad."

✴✴✴

55

As I read Carol's journal notes I questioned how her psychic gifts could be called 'gifts' at all and wondered if there was an upside to living with these special attributes. Then I found another entry in 'My Poems' dated July 94 where Carol mentioned three dreams and three 'visits' from Mark. In the first dream, Carol could see her son smiling and she wanted to run into his outstretched arms, but she could not get there. It inspired the following verses, entitled Mark.

In dreams I see you standing
With arms extended wide
I want to run and hug you
To keep you by my side

I just can't seem to get there
You smile and fade away
I have a need to hold you
In dreams I'll find a way

Carol wrote the following about the next two dreams: "I had a second one and Mark's look was sad — for me. His expression seemed to say 'Aw Mom.' Tears sprung from his eyes and flowed like a river, so sad for me. I awoke drenched.

"In a third dream came the meaning of the first dream. I saw Mark, arms outstretched, he walked towards me, I ran and hugged him. Oh God, I could feel 'the Markie Hug' so deep and he rocked with me like always. The dream was not like a movie, it's like I was there or him here, I awoke and could still feel the hug. Thank you Mark."

Carol's 'angel' artwork

THE PRICE OF DUTY

"...The Price of Duty follows the soldiers of the 1 Combat Engineer Regiment in their daily work of destroying or disarming some of the hundreds of thousands of anti-tank mines, anti-personnel mines and booby-traps that have been planted in the Balkans since civil war broke out in 1991. As we see in dramatic close-ups, it's a painstaking job with great personal risk, requiring nerves of steel and unwavering trust among soldiers. It's a job that cost Canadian Peacekeeper Mark Isfeld his life."

National Film Board Synopsis of The Price of Duty

After Mark's death the NFB film director Garth Pritchard asked if they could cover the story to the end. The Isfelds gave their permission for the crew to attend the funeral and to wrap up the documentary as the director saw fit. The result was a one-hour documentary called *The Price of Duty*, part of a three-part Protection Force Series about Canadian peacekeeping in the former Yugoslavia.

It had to be difficult for the Isfelds to attend the screening of the documentary less than a year after Mark's death. Although still emotionally raw, Carol and Brian said they had to be there. They sat in Calgary's Jubilee Auditorium along with an audience of 3,000 and watched the story of 1CER unfold before their eyes. It told of the professionalism of 1CER and of the risky business of disarming mines in the former Yugoslavia. There were close-ups of Mark de-mining alongside his Sapper buddies. As well, there was a short clip of Mark's amateur footage of him dismantling a landmine which he had filmed for his family the year before. With Mark's death, the documentary had taken a profound twist, and heartbreaking scenes of his loved ones grieving at the funeral emphasized the real cost of soldiering. Carol and Brian praised Garth Pritchard for doing such a fine job. Not only had this film supported their resolution to not let this soldier be forgotten, it served to educate Canadians to the true price of duty.

***

It was at the *Price of Duty* screening where Carol met Jan Randall, the man who had composed the music track for the film.

I interviewed Jan about meeting the Isfelds. "Here's a documentary about war. Here's Carol giving these dolls. I was bowled over that everyone who saw this film would be moved profoundly by these parents. Don't know how I knew but the first thing I said to her was that 'I feel very close to you.' Perhaps I'd been crying, having trouble doing the music because it (their story) was so moving."

Carol asked for Jan's address and sent him an Izzy Doll in appreciation for his musical contribution to the film.

"I wanted to do something," continued Jan, "I intuitively ask people for things." So he asked Carol to send him one of her poems. Carol chose to forward *My Son, Our Sons,* and with minimal adaptations to the lyrics, Jan composed a piano arrangement with a classical flavour and recorded it with singer Sherri Sommerville.

Brian and Carol were impressed, and Brian added the track to Mark's online memorial site.

Most artists hope to reach beyond their own audience of friends and family, and Carol had hoped that one day one of her poems would be published either as a song or in a book of poetry and move someone as deeply as she felt writing it. Thanks to Jan Randall, *My Son, Our Sons* was now recorded as a song. Her poem was also awarded the International War Veterans Poetry Archives (IWVPA) Double Tap Award for War Poetry and as she had wished, the poem she had written as a birthday present for Mark would indeed continually reach people.

"We are each of us angels with only one wing, and we can only fly by embracing one another."

Luciano de Crescenzo

The Isfelds remained committed to their resolution that Mark's life would not be forgotten. Carol busied her hands crocheting Izzy Dolls and giving interviews. The story of the Izzy Doll charmed the public and more crafters revelled in the idea of using their talents to create dolls that would bring a smile to a child in need. Many of the knitters accessed the doll pattern included on Mark's memorial site as well as a print-out of a small card with Mark's picture and a few words about him which could be attached with yarn when a doll was completed.

Carol referred to the knitters as her angels, based on her personal belief that angels would appear when there was a need. Brian talked about the progression of the doll phenomenon: "Slowly the idea caught on, as news stories remarked on her (Carol's) program. … Hundreds of women with time on their hands – mostly elderly and most of them mothers – began making these "Izzy Dolls" to send to soldiers for distribution to kids. I have watched those who've become involved in Carol's brainchild regain interest, energy and enthusiasm to help others – a rebirth of energy."

In 1998 Billy Willbond, founder of ICROSS Canada, asked the Isfelds if the Izzy Dolls could be distributed to the children in the most destitute areas of the world. The dolls would be used as the packaging for fragile medical equipment then distributed to the local children at the point of arrival.

Brian explained, "It was immensely satisfying when the organization, International Community for the Relief of Starvation and Suffering (ICROSS) Canada, chose the Izzy Doll as their icon, making thousands of these dolls to be used to pack fragile medical supplies destined for the poorest of the poor in poor countries around the world." Comments and emails from soldiers and ICROSS Canada workers alike poured in. Carol truly felt Mark's legacy was having a positive impact. The Izzy Doll was a hit, just as Mark had said. By now hundreds, even thousands, of Canadians volunteering to knit or package or pick-up, were feeling the glow of goodwill that Mark had felt.

From Carol's perspective the need for dolls outweighed the supply. It was a worry that brought her again to tears and on her knees in prayer. Unbeknown to her, a widow in eastern Ontario, who was to become a dear friend and ally, had heard about the Izzy Dolls and felt guided to contact Carol with an inspiration.

In 2005 Shirley O'Connell, a member of the Order of the Eastern Star (OES), proposed a plan whereby OES members would knit and collect Izzy Dolls. With 131 chapters in Ontario alone it would significantly boost the number of dolls, a clear and undisputed answer to Carol's prayers. As Carol put it, Shirley seemed to come from out of the blue, like another angel arriving to meet a need.

Brian observed that as Carol told Mark's story and promoted the dolls, she was educating civilians about soldiers: "Carol worked tirelessly to preserve Mark's memory by continuing with her project of the Izzy Doll (and) at the same time bringing awareness to those citizens in civilian clothing across our great country that military people are indeed living, breathing individuals with emotions, desires, and compassion for other human beings in less fortunate circumstances than themselves, with families of their own, rather than just automatons in uniforms with weapons and tools of war." '

"We all know no one hears a tree fall in the forest. You can feel pain, see pain but no one hears a heart break."

From Carol's address at the second meeting of State's Parties,
Geneva Switzerland 2000

The Isfelds grieved the finality a landmine had wrought, robbing their son of a promising future. Repeatedly Mark had reinforced the importance of his job, that for every landmine he lifted, a life was saved. His words became Carol and Brian's guiding mantra and they joined the Canadian Landmine Foundation. It is a registered charity with a mission to raise awareness and funds to end the human and economic suffering caused by anti-personnel landmines. (www. clearlandmines.com) They traveled to Ottawa where the international landmine ban treaty was signed and to Geneva Switzerland for follow up meetings of the State's Parties.

Their eyes were opened to the tens of millions of anti-personnel landmines still infecting lands no longer at war laying in wait to maim or kill the next innocent victim. As well, other unexploded ordnance (UXO) abandoned after ceasefires and left stockpiled in buildings or cellars could be detonated by accident causing injury or death. Landmines, bombs, bullets, grenades and other remnants of war are too plentiful to quantify, but human casualties can be estimated and the statistics are shocking.

Roméo A. Dallaire, Carol Isfeld and MP John Duncan

It is estimated that 25,000 people every year are killed or maimed by UXO. It affects the lives of entire families. Women and children are frequent victims. Death robs families of breadwinners and careers. The injured become a burden for others, losing their dignity through dependence and an inability to work.

Carol and Brian met the human faces behind the statistics: men, women, children, amputees, the blind, the crippled. They heard the true stories of human carnage similar to the sights Mark told of in his letters. Carol related that the children who were disabled by landmines "really affected me" and that "anyone who met a child who had been in a landmine accident would look at things in a different light." She admitted that the perseverance and courage shown by the survivors of landmines had given her strength to deal with her own loss.

Brian joined the Landmine Survivor Network, which organized peer support and hospital visits and helped with job training for those left disabled. It advocates for landmine bans as well as for international awareness and aid for survivors.

The legacy Mark left was more than the gifting of Izzy Dolls. His job as a Sapper opened the eyes of his parents to the tremendous need to eradicate landmines. Carol and Brian agreed with Scott Fairweather of the Canadian Landmine Foundation that humanitarian mine action is an act of peacemaking. Therefore, included in this book is a chapter called *Landmines: The Cowardly Soldier*. It details how the Isfelds contributed to the movement to ban landmines, as well as to the progress and achievements of the world organizations that continue to work toward the elimination of landmines on this planet.

"Do what you can, with what you have, where you are.... Far and away the best prize that life offers is the chance to work hard, at work worth doing."

Theodore Roosevelt

The spotlight was the last place Carol would have chosen to be. As a homemaker more content in her garden than in the public limelight, she found it odd that people would be interested in what she had to say. But an inner drive to tell Mark's story forced her to step out of her comfort zone, and in doing so she met many high profile people.

Brian wrote this about his wife's modesty:

"Unexpectedly for Carol, the Izzy Doll phenomenon led to her rubbing shoulders with public figures. She never realized they were as much in awe of her as she was of them. She met Paul McCartney, who identified with her project. She dined with governor-generals and met with senior politicians. She received letters of support from Diana, Princess of Wales, and Queen Noor of Jordan. She received the gratitude and admiration of senior military officers. Through it all, she never aspired to be anything other than "mom" to those who loved her, and always thought of others before herself."

There were particular introductions she would remember fondly. Carol and Brian had followed the events surrounding Lt.-Gen. Romeo Dallaire, the man who agonized over the plight of the people he was sent to Rwanda to protect. Carol considered him a hero and felt honoured to shake his hand, get a hug, and have a photo taken with him.

Judy fondly remembers the one time her sister did get a little bit giddy about meeting a celebrity — one of Carol's teenage idols from the 1960s. It was at an anti-landmine event in Geneva, Switzerland. "Carol was very unassuming. It tickled her to meet all the people she did and she handled it like a pro. Never did she gloat or think she was special or brag. (Except) maybe once, (about) being hugged and kissed by Paul McCartney, not

Heather Mills holds an Izzy Doll and her then husband Paul McCartney touches Carol's shoulder

once but twice. (It) was the thrill of her life. It was the only time she bragged, and as I write this I am smiling because I remember it so well … When she started making these dolls it was not for notoriety, nor did she seek it. She was just being Carol, finding a way to help."

MY MOTHER, OUR MOTHERS

"I would rather have all my twelve about me tonight than all your pilgrimages, so I would."
Parting words of Mrs. Charlotte Wood, Winnipeg, Manitoba as she embarked on the Vimy
Pilgrimage, 1936

All mothers and spouses of our fallen receive the Silver Cross Medal (also called the Memorial Cross.) It is given to all mothers and spouses to pay tribute to the lives of their sons and daughters, husbands and wives of the Canadian Forces who died while in service of their country. In 2000 the Royal Canadian Legion selected Carol as Canada's Silver Cross Mother, which meant placing a wreath at the National War Memorial during the Remembrance Day Ceremony in Ottawa on behalf of these mothers. It was an emotional trip, yet a remarkable one that boosted the Isfelds' patriotism and gratitude for the sacrifices of our soldiers and their families throughout our country's history.

The Silver Cross medal was instituted in 1919. Mrs. Charlotte Wood became the first Silver Cross Mother in 1935. The following year, along with thousands of other Canadians, she travelled to France for the unveiling of Canada's Vimy War Memorial by King Edward VIII. Her parting words to the press, (above) that she would rather have her children around her than any pilgrimage, echoed the sentiment of other recipients of the Silver Cross Medal, past and present.

***

It was an ordinary morning when the Silver Cross Medal arrived at the Isfeld home — ordinary, but unforgettable. The mail had arrived as it always had but that day's delivery from Ottawa evoked anger in Brian and brought Carol to tears. No doubt a clerical error, but a painful stupid error nonetheless; the package was actually addressed to Mark.

Now unwrapped and resting on the living room table, the medal, which was supposed to be a memento of personal loss and sacrifice, looked worn out and tarnished. Not as official as one might expect of an institution proud of the 'spit and polish' ritual that exemplified discipline and high standards. Obviously minted in large quantities and stored over long periods of time, it appeared that due diligence was neglected before sending it out.

The pride associated with the arrival of Carol's Silver Cross Medal had quickly faded into disbelief. Carol was numb. Brian wrestled with the notion of how many other mothers, recipients of this medal of tribute, saw it arrive in Canada Post along with their phone bill and grocery flyers. How many others saw it arrive improperly addressed and tired and tarnished looking, to boot. Outraged at the unnecessary emotional stress the oversight caused his wife, and determined to protect other mothers in the future, Brian picked up the phone. He would take care of it in his own way, going right to the top: to his Member of Parliament for Vancouver Island North, John Duncan.

62

John Duncan recalls, "Brian was furious. But as was so typical, Brian found a way to turn his anger into a catalyst for positive change."

Working together, citizen and parliamentarian achieved their goal of changing the way the Silver Cross was issued. John goes on to say, "A new procedure was put in place whereby the Canadian Forces would present the medal to loved ones in an official ceremony, which is a much more appropriate way to honour the sacrifices made by the families of our soldiers, sailors and airmen."

An emotional low-key ceremony was held at CFB Comox to officially present Carol with her Silver Cross Medal. Carol had insisted their MP be invited because, after all, "there would be no ceremony without John Duncan." The Isfelds and their MP collaborated on many issues and were an example of how democracy can accomplish so much when citizen and politician work together to bring change.

***

Years before, as a military wife raising small children, Carol had tuned in to the televised annual Remembrance Ceremony broadcast from our nation's capital. She said she watched the dignified, aging Silver Cross Mother perform her role and wondered, because it was a relatively peaceful time in the world, who would represent the mothers and ensure remembrance of our soldiers' sacrifices in the future.

But Carol needn't have wondered. It has been ninety-one years since the first Memorial Cross (Silver Cross Medal) was presented and seventy-four years since Mrs. Charlotte Wood laid a wreath at London's Westminster Abbey on behalf of all the mourning mothers of Canadian soldiers from World War I. Soldiers continue to die in subsequent wars and missions and mourning never ends. And now, ironically, Carol was playing the role of Silver Cross Mother herself. And she said what other Silver Cross Mothers have said; that they would gladly relinquish this honour if it meant not having to lose their loved one. Carol had reiterated to me what Mrs. Wood had imparted; both of them wishing there would never have to be a need for a medal, remembrance ceremonies, or pilgrimages at all.

***

Brian and the Silver Cross Mother arrived in Ottawa on November 9. They checked into their room at the regal Chateau Laurier, which overlooks the Cenotaph and is just up the street from the Parliament Buildings. They discussed their schedule for the next few days with Dominion Command Ted Keast (RCL). It included guided tours, media interviews, meetings with dignitaries and more. The itinerary was full and would be hectic, but when it was over the Isfelds would feel they had been on a pilgrimage of sorts, a heartfelt and spiritual journey leaving them with, as Brian described, "a life time of memories of our Remembrance Day 2000."

Brian, 'Smokey' Smith, and Carol

Early the next morning, November 10, they arrived at the Parliament Buildings for their first tour. The great halls were alive with historical presence; they are the heart of our democracy where bills are declared law for Canadian citizens spread out over a vast land between three oceans. This is also where foreign policy and decisions of national defence are made, committing our soldiers to missions at home and abroad, in combat, peace, or in response to natural disasters. Every Canadian is inexplicably tied to these rooms filled with policy makers and politicians making decisions that affect us all.

Carol viewed the future in the faces of the winners of the Remembrance essay, poetry, and poster contests, who were included in their entourage. Brian relished the past, meeting centenarian Paul Metivier, a survivor of the "war to end all wars." He spoke at length with Ernest Alvia "Smokey" Smith VC CM, Canada's last surviving Victoria Cross winner. The morning continued with a visit to the Senate and an education on the workings of Canada's Upper Chamber.

Another location of great interest to the Isfelds was the Memorial Chapel in the Peace Tower. It is the repository for the Six Books of Remembrance that commemorate Canadians who died in the service of their country during the South African War and Nile Expedition (1884-1885), both WI and WWII, and Korea. Ironically, as of the year 2000, there was no book that recorded Mark Isfeld's name or any of the Peacekeepers or soldiers killed in active duty since WWII and the Korean conflicts. It seemed nonsensical that the son of this year's Silver Cross Mother was not recognized in the nation's hallowed books: the most sacred place of Remembrance. This, too, would be rectified.

Taking advantage of the fact that Parliament was not in session, the tour was led into the House of Commons. Carol paused in the giant Speaker's Chair that dwarfed her figure while Brian snapped another photo for the family album.

The morning spent, they began their afternoon agenda with a stroll through the War Museum. A Museum of war exhibits, combat artefacts, battle dioramas and much more but, paradoxically, it also holds the evidence of the sacrifice of Canadians who have conscientiously contributed to peace in the world. Ottawa's War Museum is an outstanding example of this and was a 'must see again' for a history buff like Brian.

Carol and Brian were fond of this museum because of a heart-warming experience they had on a previous visit. While browsing the artefacts and perusing the displays, they had turned a corner and stopped in their tracks. Before their eyes was a very familiar face — a life size photo of their son. It was Mark on his third tour clearing mines in the Croatian countryside. Shock turned into elation; they approached the staff to let them know the soldier's name and his story. Coincidentally the exhibition was titled "We'll Meet Again." This chance meeting of parents and son and the introduction of the Unknown Soldier to the staff added a human dimension to the museum's exhibit and reinforced to the Isfelds that once again their son would not be forgotten.

Brian also visited a display honouring Mrs. Charlotte Susan Wood and read about her life. She had stepped into mothering six boys all under the age of eight when she married widower Frederick Wood. Together they had another five sons and a daughter for a total of twelve children. At the onset of WWI their eldest boys enlisted, soon followed by their other sons, two of whom were underage. Five were killed and two were seriously wounded but survived the war.

Like so many mothers trying to make sense out of the devastation and loss, Carol Isfeld included, Mrs. Wood channelled her grief into service for others, tending to the needs of disabled veterans and grieving families. An active legion member, she contributed towards acts of commemorating the fallen to ensure the sacrifice of their lives would not be forgotten.

There were many opportunities for media interviews, and the coverage on television, radio and newspaper reached the ears of mothers across Canada. The schedule was hectic, but in many ways a delight for the senses with fine cuisine at luncheons and formal dinners in rooms with exquisite décor. Gifts and plaques were presented to Carol as the SCM. She reciprocated by giving gifts of Izzy Dolls.

The Isfelds spoke highly of the consideration shown to them and were deeply touched by the empathy shown by the dignitaries, workers and aids. Experiencing historic Ottawa was an exploration and an education of the pioneers and their descendents who had built, led and sacrificed for our nation. From Politician to soldier, farmers and labourers and many more, Carol and Brian regarded their stories with deep admiration and homage.

***

65

The Isfelds awoke on Remembrance Day in their sixth floor suite of the Chateau Laurier. The elegant window dressings were opened wide, framing the little figures at the Cenotaph below, busy readying the area for the ceremonies later that morning.

Their son was foremost in their thoughts. The stories and images of the previous day's events had galvanized an appreciation for the contributions by so many soldiers and their families throughout our history. Today a nation would stand together, remember and mourn united.

There was a chill in the morning air. A respectful applause welcomed them as they stepped out of their official car onto the red carpet. The medallion, in the shape of a cross with a laurel wreath, hung from a wide ribbon of solid purple, bright against her dark wool coat. Carol stood beside Canada's dignitaries, Prime Minister Chretien and his wife, Aline, Governor General Adrienne Clarkson and her husband John Ralston Saul, Chief of Defence Staff and the Dominion President. She took her turn in sequence and positioned the wreath on the cenotaph on behalf of Canadian mothers and widows, the reason she was here.

A celestial chorus of voices was a perfect, contemplative backdrop for the thousands in attendance. A colour party and Pipe Band led a procession of wide-eyed cadets, stoic Veterans, blue-bereted Peacekeepers, and RCMP in blood red tunics — a marching metaphor of our past, present and future.

***

Carol continued to receive attention and awards for the Izzy Doll project. In April 2006 the Right Honourable Michaëlle Jean, Governor General of Canada, presented the Meritorious Service Medal to Carol and Brian for their initiation of the Izzy Doll. A flurry of media coverage resulted again, which led more Canadians to commit to making dolls. Carol was pleased about the Izzy Doll story reaching so many, but she could not get her head around the fact people thought she should receive an award for doing something that came so naturally. Brian explained it this way: "Although she was well aware of the impact of Mark's story and the phenomenon the Izzy Doll created, she thought it was 'weird' that she would win a medal for making a doll for her son."

Carol, Prime Minister Chrétien and wife Aline

Brian and Carol dine with Adrienne Clarkson

The Isfelds regularly celebrated special occasions like Easter and New Year's Eve with their friends Dave and Lynn Breese. Lynn explained that Carol made you feel special and was always exuberant with praise; how lovely their home was, how delicious the meal. And when Carol hosted one of her favourite spaghetti dinners, it had to be fun. She would whip up two new desserts as mouth-watering props for Brian and Dave to act out their routine of competing for the largest piece.

I experienced Carol's warmth and hospitality when I visited the Isfelds in Courtney, B.C. in 2006 to introduce the Izzy Doll song I had written. Brian had taxied me from the airport to their home and it was almost noon when we arrived. Nestled in beside the flowing Puntledge River, their small acreage was thick with trees, ferns and cultivated shrubbery and flowers. It was Carol's sanctuary, the place she loved to be when she wasn't engaged in painting or pottery in her ceramic studio.

Carol greeted me at the door smiling, and I felt at ease and liked her instantly. She had prepared lunch; delicate finger sandwiches and tea, laid out upon a lace tablecloth. Generous with her time, she led me into her world, wanting me to understand Mark's story and the beginnings of the Izzy Doll.

To clear up any misconception I may have had, she pointed out that many parents sent gifts and packages for their soldiers and that, "we were not the only ones." She proceeded to tell me this story: A young soldier received a box of goodies from his parents, probably in response to his concern for the forlorn and needy kids he had met. It was filled with toys, crayons and other stuff the children were sure to like. He stood and watched them edge their way up to the box and reach inside with anticipation, big grins spread across their little faces. A young girl with an infant in her arms patiently waited until all the items had disappeared and then approached the soldier. With disappointment in his voice he said, "I'm sorry but there is nothing left." The very young mother replied, "Please, may I have the box to put my baby in?"

Carol emphasized that there were many such stories that never reached the Canadian public. They were important stories she said would educate us to the world outside our safe and prosperous cocoon and to the realities our soldiers were exposed to regularly.

We stood in her ceramic studio surrounded by her art tools, kiln, moulds, brushes, and paints. She sighed as she spoke about her family trait of premonitions and dreams. She said she had accepted this psychic gift but wasn't always sure what to do with it. We walked into her living room, where framed water color scenes of wildlife and garden flowers decorated the walls.

She pointed to the collection of porcelain and glass angels that lined the mantle and shelves and said she believed in angels and that they appear when you needed them. Alongside the angels stood miniature elephants, another collectable she treasured, with trunks extended skyward, a sign of good fortune.

Feelings can overwhelm a mother with a buffet of mixed emotions, and so they did with Carol. On one hand she was relieved that her son had pursued a career that gave him a sense of purpose. On the other hand, a career choice that took him into hostile, far reaches of the planet, working with explosive devices, was worrisome for her, to say the least. Carol told me she felt a kinship for families of Peacekeepers as well as policemen and women who are put in harm's way serving their country. Reaching inside her handwritten book of poems, she pulled out a photo and a newspaper article she had stored there. It was about four RCMP officers who were shot and killed in March 2005 while conducting a raid on a marijuana grow-op near Mayerthorpe, Alberta. She told me she mourned for them and that she prayed for their families.

When Corporal Daniel Gunther was killed in an unprovoked attack from an anti-tank rocket, near Buci, Bosnia, in June 1993 Carol she said she grieved for his family, also. Although they had never met, they shared a bond that only families of soldiers could understand. She sent her poem *My Son, Our Sons* to Daniel's parents, Peter Gunther and Dominique Leiba-Gunther, in the hope that they would know they were not alone.

The phone rang and broke Carol's train of thought. Although it was easily within reach she told me that Brian would answer it. Every telephone ring reminded her of when Mark would call, and she explained that she couldn't watch the videos Mark had made, either, because to see and hear him hurt too much. The Izzy Doll had undergone changes too. "After Mark's death, I just couldn't bring myself to give them a face." She added that other knitters or even the children could add a face if they wished.

Carol was a giver, content to bring a smile to friend or stranger. As I was about to leave she handed me my own Izzy Doll wearing a blue beret. There was a handwritten note attached: *Phyllis! Keep up the good work, May your steps be safe. What we do for ourself dies with us, but inspires others. What we do for others lives on forever! To make a memory — you had to be there." God Bless you and yours. Carol Isfeld.*

Carol had certainly made me aware that a soldier's sacrifice is his family's sacrifice, too, and my viewpoint had shifted in other ways as well. I no longer saw the image of the stiff-jawed stereotypical soldier who was stoically resilient, even robotic in performing duties. I began to see each soldier holistically. More than bones and muscle and calculated missions, they have relationships; loved ones, opinions and thoughts, all of which are equally susceptible to stress, damage, and breakage just like a physical injury. Carol's personal experience deserved my respect and an open mind. She summed it all up in one line, "Whether you agree or disagree with the politicians, support our men and women who put their lives on the line."

Hearing Mark's story was an eye opener and I felt pride knowing men like Mark were excellent ambassadors who represent Canada's values abroad. Much later I found a little angel Carol had slipped into my purse. The tiny porcelain angel with gold tipped wings playing a fiddle now sits on my desk in front of my computer and still brings a smile to my face. I wonder if Carol would be pleased to know I am writing their story. It was something no one could have predicted at the time. Well, maybe Carol could have.

"My wife Carol was a phenomenon in my eyes, and the eyes of many who had the opportunity to encounter her methodology of instilling in many people across this land a feeling of usefulness to their fellow humans, yet at the same time drawing the focus of her endeavours to ultimately be a tribute to the memory of her son, and mine, at the same time giving hope, sense of worth, and purpose to many elderly people who knit the Izzy Doll."
Brian Isfeld Tribute to Carol August 17, 2007

I think Carol knew that 2007 was the beginning of her last year on this earthly plane. Her sister, Judy, recalls, "The winter before she died Carol called me and said she felt she was dying. She was going around the house leaving notes on all her stuff. Naturally I tried to tell her she was just feeling blue, forgetting she had a way about her and her premonitions were usually right on."

With pen in hand and her little blue book of poems opened wide, she edited her work, adding dates and notes for clarification should someone in the future read its pages. Then she followed up with the list below, noting the accomplishments and her feelings since her son's death thirteen years ago. It was a reflection of the exceptional opportunities as well as the countless ways her son would now be remembered. It did not make the pain go away, but knowing her son would not be forgotten comforted her.

God Help Me, I'm Lonely. It's 2007 - January. Been reading all the poems. I have been through every emotion over and over. One illness triggers another - stress I hear. I've seen the dolls honoured so many ways - been to Ottawa, Geneva, Ottawa twice more. Seen a bridge - Creston "Izzy Bridge" made and dedicated to Mark by the Engineers at Trail B.C. A school in Courtenay named after Mark. A statue in Calgary (old Army Base) Peacekeepers Park: a peacekeeper handing a child a doll. My doll is now in bronze, every stitch depicted. Second field to clear of mines in Mark's name near where he died in Kakma, Croatia. An offshoot of my doll "Izzy comfort doll" sent by the thousands to kids dying of aids - thanks to 'willy' willbond - Victoria (British Columbia).

Visited the institute of peace and "the wall" in washington. Been to the signing of the Landmine Treaty in '97 etc. etc. And all because of Mark, his nature, his kindness and the Doll he requested to keep going. I'm honoured and humbled and unable to put together a poem. It's been said - now I pray for peace, cry for new hurting mothers and keep making Dolls!"

In April of 2007 Carol survived a heart attack and was soon back at home recovering nicely, knitting needles in hand and Mikey, her trusted four-legged companion, snuggled in beside her on the sofa. But by August, Carol was suffering with regular and severe abdominal pain. She was admitted into the hospital and scheduled for emergency surgery the next day. She never made it to the operating room. Carol died late that evening, Wednesday, August 15, 2007.

"I truly believe that her project was predestined to become a vehicle of pleasure to many, to the knitters, to the crocheters, and ultimately to the young recipients of the labours of love generated by the many people across the land who participated, and who will continue to participate in the producing and distributing of the Izzy Doll, and now that she is at peace with her maker and once more joined with her son Mark, she has finally reached the goal that was intended for her all along."

Brian Isfeld, Tribute to Carol August 17, 2007

Friday morning at the Isfeld family home, Brian discovered a single crimson rose. He called it miraculous; it was blooming right outside Carol's bedroom window. Carol had written in her Book of Poems that a red rose was a symbol of love and now, as if pre-ordered by his wife, here it grew reaching toward the sun and the heavens as if promising that love transcends death and lives on.

CHAPTER 3

BRIAN ISFELD, MSM, CD

OCTOBER 5, 1939 – JANUARY 20, 2008

Little boy Brian

BRIAN AND PAT

Nov. 2000.

In Loving Memory

Dear Poppa,

I miss you today more than
these words can say. We are here now,
as a family and as a country, because
of your love for us, because of your
courage. I will never forget what you
did for us. I love you. M. xoxoxo

MAN OF LOGIC

"Seriously, do you understand what I am saying? Is it clear and unfettered enough to get the picture, that there is no difference between Peacekeepers and soldiers; they are one and the same in Canada? (This is not necessarily true in other countries such as Norway and Sweden who DO have standing forces dedicated to UN action only). I sent this to Jim (Davis) for his comments. Should have some by tomorrow. Cheers, Ernest Hemingway."

An excerpt from Brian's e-mail to me in July 2007.
(He was trying to de-mystify the role of the Canadian Peacekeeper.)

Multicoloured gems spilled out of Brian's travel suitcase that sat open on the carpeted floor. Dolls with smiling faces and heads with wild-yarned hairdos seemed ready to play. These were a recent shipment of newly knitted Izzy Dolls en route to the arms of needy children. I snapped a photo and smiled, but it wasn't because the dolls were so cute. It seemed to me incongruous that a retired military man, a collector of war memorabilia and a war history buff, was toting a suitcase devoted to dolls. But I knew his story and once again was witnessing the compelling command of these little toys to affect even a tough veteran like Brian Isfeld.

Brian had arrived in Calgary for the 2007 Peacekeepers Day, an annual August ceremony that had been held in Peacekeepers Park since the park's unveiling in 2004. Carol and Brian had attended on that momentous occasion and Carol would have been here with Brian if she had been feeling well enough to travel. She urged her husband to go and to take lots of pictures.

Both happy and traumatic events had aligned to bring Brian to Calgary on this particular weekend chock full of scheduled events. Hindsight is 20/20, and looking back at his life and this particular weekend of meetings and encounters, it seemed to me that providence was preparing him for the imminent good-byes of the days and months ahead.

***

Brian Isfeld had chosen his career early in life. Enlisting in the Royal Canadian Air Force in 1958, he trained as an Airborne Electronics System Operator and served for more than thirty years. He flew in the Argus, which for its era was the most advanced anti-submarine aircraft in the world, then served onboard the Aurora. His job required extreme concentration for long periods of time within a small space.

73

The crew of either sixteen or twelve respectively, patrolled and observed the Canadian shorelines and mid-ocean during the cold war. They tracked submarines that could be considered potential threats to Canada's sovereignty and were deployed in operations in allied countries as needed. They participated in search and rescue operations and recorded and provided data for our fisheries. Brian spoke of a career that was rewarding and that had satisfied his thirst for travel and adventure, a career template that might have easily inspired Mark toward the military.

My first impression of Brian came from the correspondence I had initiated with the Isfelds about The Izzy Doll song I was writing. His emails were cordial and depicted a husband and father who was excited to contribute towards a piece of music based on his son's story. He was generous with information and sent excerpts from Mark's letters, bits of Carol's poetry, his father Arilius' writings, and some essays of his own.

We established a rapport as I asked questions about the military and Peacekeepers. Our correspondence expanded to Canadian history and he responded with attachments, web addresses, and titles of books. In a very short time he began speaking candidly and had included my name on his joke list, which to me was a sign that I had graduated from stranger into the ranks of his mixed bag of friends. I welcomed the opportunity to meet the Isfelds in their home on subsequent events.

A self-reliant man, logic ruled his perspective. He was a force eager to take on a challenge and competent at doing so. His only sibling, Pat, explained that their parents Arilius and Steinem Isfeld taught their children the value of independence and to, "take care of ourselves — no one else will."

Pat described her brother as a realist. "He appeared to be brusque and rough but my brother had common sense. He was in touch with reality and what was going on in the world." Married to a base commander, Pat was familiar with the rationale of the military and its regimental life style. Brother and sister shared a mutual understanding and she explained that this was why her brother trusted her judgment.

Dave Breese, who served in the same squadron as Brian, said his friend of almost forty years was guarded about his personal life and protective of his family. Dave explained that Brian was not the man you saw on the outside and that he had great depth on the inside. Both Pat and Dave described Brian as a complex individual, even an enigma. Boastful of his next of kin, he was rarely boastful of his own talents. Very intelligent, he was often unaware of the sensibilities of others and his affect on them.

Well read, Brian had respect for the contributions of generations past. His fascination with history and the stories behind the antiques he collected is evidence of this. I asked about the markings on one of the Byzantine coins in his collection and he forwarded pages of information about the reigning Byzantine emperor at the time and what life was like during that era. It was not just a coin, he explained, but an artefact, once held in the bare hand of a living, breathing person of a long-gone era and a clue into the past that should not be permitted to be forgotten.

Words were to Brian what the artist's medium was to Carol. Arilius, a teacher and principal, had instructed his children in the power of the pen to influence and to wield change. Brian created inspirational speeches for presentations and wrote dynamic letters that could sway politicians and high-ranking military men. The pen was a super-tool in his hands; it won him the admiration of powerful people and gratitude from those he helped.

Anything of interest to Brian was recorded with words or with photos. He was a rock-hound and mineral collector and traveled to obscure beaches climbing rock formations to gather specimens of agates, amethyst, gypsum, jasper and fossils, often with his sons. He photographed and catalogued his finds and even made jewellery from the most promising polished samples.

With special equipment he cut into the rocks exposing their intricate rings and generations of their history. Akin to a lottery win, he would occasionally reap a reward. Inside the dullest and least significant specimen shone brilliant and magnificent coloured quartz crystals formed and released as Brian said, "by the relentless forces of nature." I likened the exercise of his hobby to the adage; one shouldn't judge a book by its cover. Brian came across as rough around the edges. He chose the comfort of T-shirt and baggy pants over pleated pants and coordinated golf shirts and he often opted to leave out his ill-fitting dentures, which he called bothersome and painful. So consequently his exterior gave a first impression that didn't represent Brian's great depth and character, and he was very aware of it. In one of his essays he even admits to being "a wee bit like Oscar" of the Odd Couple. "I am the type of guy that can take a suit that cost $3,000 and by the simple act of donning it, make it look like a cast off from the back of the local dump, newly found. Tailors hate me."

During the years the Isfeld family spent in Nova Scotia, Brian wrote a walkthrough guiding the reader through small coastal towns and beaches along the southern shore of Fundy in search of their "super gem." This can still be found on their website, www.rockhound.com. I'm sure he succeeded in convincing many to travel the trails to uncover hidden treasures in the Canadian landscape.

Not a religious man, nature was Brian's cathedral. Communing with the elements on land or sea was his place of contemplation and paradoxically an arena of competition and ability. Tyee, a word from the coastal aboriginal language meaning the chief, distinguishes a Chinook salmon of thirty pounds or more, and those fishermen who boated such a catch would become a member of the Tyee Club. Brian fished the Tyee Pool between Campbell River and Quadra Island following the unique rules set out by the club. These rules can be found on their web site (www.tyeeclub.org): "Tyee fishing here is different. You'll fish quietly in small, classic row boats. No motors are allowed in the Tyee pool. The rower will slip the boat into the currents and eddies of the pool, keeping a basic plug or spoon beating in the current. The angler must stay focused on the action of the lure as it is felt in the hand as much as being seen by the beating of the rod tip. With the slightest change in the beat, the hook must be set, fast and hard. The battle with a Pacific Chinook Salmon is on — anything can happen!"

Brian landed his prized Tyee in 1992 during his very first experience in the pool, and the over 30 pound catch guaranteed his membership in the Tyee Club. He returned to the mystique of the pool, as he called it, and to the natural solitude where, no doubt, he spent time ruminating and creating his best jokes. I can picture Brian in my mind's eye, in a scene from Hemmingway's *The Old Man and the Sea*, a silhouette against the early morning sunrise in his self-directed quest to land his next behemoth salmon.

"Dad was a pragmatic guy who when posed with the philosophical question, 'Do you view the cup as half empty or half full?' would reply 'It's a half a glass of water, what more do you want to know?'"

Leigh Isfeld about his Dad

Everyone recognized that Brian was highly competent in his field of interest and in fighting a cause. He maintained an objectivity that, he would proudly point out, was not clouded with the emotional. But Leigh identified the weakness that was his father's Achilles heel. "My dad could give you the information but he had two left feet with feelings."

Leigh elaborates on growing up with a dad who was not a natural leader, even though he was always educating someone about something. He indirectly taught by "pushing," as his son explains with an anecdote from his youth: Leigh had been watching his father skilfully fly-tying — the art of producing flies to replicate the prey of specific species of fish the fisherman sought to catch. It was an art Brian had spent years mastering. Repeatedly throwing questions at his father prompted what Leigh says were his father's three favourite words, "Look it up!" It was akin to throwing down the gauntlet and his dad completed the challenge with, "If you want to learn how to do this, read a book or take a class."

A son could easily interpret his father as being uninterested in him, but Leigh said that he understood it was his dad's way. He accepted the challenge of the push and in time Leigh did read a book and take a class. Sure enough they were speaking on the same level — at least with fly-fishing.

Whether conscious of his style or not, Brian forced others to step up, become informed, and speak to him at his level of knowledge. There were also occasions when he had been known to admit he was wrong, and he also admired anyone who had the courage to appropriately step up to the plate and push back.

On Brian's last visit to Leigh's home in 2007 they went out for dinner with friends. Conversation was never lacking with Brian at the dinner table and Leigh wasn't surprised when his dad revived an anecdote from the family archives. Mark was about twenty at the time and he had accompanied his dad to a store in search of a certain item. Brian was abrupt with the store clerk and Mark watched the interaction with disapproval. When they got back to the car Mark scolded his father about his insensitivity, saying, "I don't want to go out with you anymore — you're a dink." Brian was not embarrassed or hurt by the poke at his lack of social graces. In fact he held his son in high regard for standing his ground and showing strength of character. Leigh pointed out that this story was among Brian's favourites and he had proudly repeated it many times over the years.

"You know, soldiers are very unusual people. on the outside, they are the hardest, most demanding people, but underneath that, they are the most human, the most feeling, the most emotionally attached people who exist."

A quote from Romeo Dallaire's father, which appeared in
Shake Hands With The Devil by Romeo Dallaire

Brian loved his family in his own unique and logical way. He could easily have written the statement, "What do you mean you don't feel loved? You are loved," minimizing the need to demonstrate it through outward acts of affection or repeatedly saying what he believed to be the obvious.

Carol could show love with thoughtful words and a hug simply because you were in the room with her. Brian's thought process, however, was similar to a computer. Feed him facts and figures and you would receive a logical output; flowery words or anything touchy–feely were unnecessary. Carol's emotions and intuitive predictions were non-fact base and difficult for Brian to process without evidence and proof. Mark, the born peacekeeper in the family, recognized their different personality styles and felt it necessary to encourage his parents to take time to show each other love.

"No one would be foolish enough to choose war over peace - In peace sons bury their fathers, but in war fathers bury their sons."

Croesus of Lydia 595 - 547 BCE

Just a week prior to Mark's homecoming in June 1994, Brian set off on a driving trip to Winnipeg making family pit-stops along the way. He visited Kelly and the kids in Chilliwack, who were excited for their soldier's return. Heading in the direction of Edmonton to visit Leigh and Glenn, he stopped at Pat's home in Leduc just south of Edmonton.

The next morning Brian and his sister had just returned from an early outing to hear the phone ringing. Carol had tried several times that fateful morning to reach her husband and was trembling as she asked for Brian. "Mark's been killed," she told Pat, "and I don't want him to hear it on the news."

Pat handed the phone to Brian, helpless to lessen the blow. Those searing moments are branded into her memory. Brian hung the phone on its cradle and Pat watched her brother walk into the next room toward the solitude he needed, and where she heard him curse in agony. The very worst predicted by Carol, and intuited by Mark, had come true only days before Mark's scheduled return. Brian wrote that their world, as they knew it, would never be the same. A man like Brian needed the facts and answers; he had to know exactly what had happened. He caught the first available plane home.

Later, he wrote about that journey, "Many thoughts go through your mind when you are captive to a situation beyond your control; sitting in what seems an interminably slow aircraft, with no ability to obtain further news, and imagining all sorts of scenarios. I finally arrived home and the tragic truth came crashing down to indelibly mark our lives for evermore."

Brian Salutes Good-Bye to his son

For Brian and Carol, the days following Mark's funeral were a balancing act of emotional endurance and expected duties. There was an interview with the NFB film crew prior to the funeral and a priority meeting Brian arranged with Mark's troop. He had to gather the facts and hear their version of the events on that fateful day.

The Brotherhood was not a myth, but truly a loyal family of men and women who were as traumatized and, as Brian said, were as deserving to share the family grief as if they were siblings with the biological right. He spoke of his great admiration and gratitude for 1CER and their commitment to his son.

Still yet another imperative that weighed on Carol and Brian's heart was Arilius. He was in a care home and it was apparent that his life was drawing to its close. He needed them too.

The swirl of activity kept the family focused on obligations and important tasks before they would realize the total impact of their loss. It was a stressful time indeed.

The evening after Mark's internment, Brian and Pat's father passed away.

MORAL RUDDERS

"My grandfather was born in Iceland, and came over in 1876/77 or so with his mother and eight or nine or ten other siblings. His father (my great grandfather) was killed by lightning while fishing in Iceland, and he himself (my dad's father), was killed by lightning fishing on lake Winnipeg in 1928. (Don't stand near me in a rainstorm!)"

Brian Isfeld, about his 'shocking' ancestry

Carol and Brian's boys spent a lot of time with grandparents on both sides of their family. All contributed to their grandsons' character and moral fibre, but there was a special connection between Mark and his paternal grandfather, Arilius. Brian explains, "Much of my father's great love for nature, the flowers and animals, the birds and bees, the love of gardening and growing things had rubbed off on Mark. They both had the same care and compassion for the very young and the elderly. Both were extremely generous in giving their time and effort to any who asked or needed help."

Leigh Isfeld called his granddad a 'horticultural renaissance man.' With an interest in a variety of pursuits, Arilius wrote poetry and prose for most of his life, leaving behind his wisdom in a legacy of writings that is as relevant today as it was then. He was a horticulturalist who experimented with grafting and he developed new species of plums and apples. He studied the insects that threatened the plants he cultivated. An avid naturalist, he would teach his grandchildren to identify birds of the meadow and sky, their distinctive calls, feeding habits and much more.

Following the example of his grandfather's love of nature, Mark prided himself as a backyard gardener and bird enthusiast. While stationed in Croatia in February 1993 he wrote his pen pal about his interests;

I enjoy working in the yard pruning trees and such… and when I'm away the weeds will play! I'm also an avid bird feeder. I know if anyone misses me, it's my little Chickadees!

In his last years, Arilius suffered from Alzheimer's disease, which slowly robbed him of his memories and his speech. Mark wrote regularly to this grandfather to try to lift the spirits of the man who taught him so much about life, nature, and the responsibilities he took seriously in his role on the world front. Mark wrote this letter while he was stationed in Camp Polom, Croatia.

Hi Grandpa,

I made this card for you 'cause we can't get any here right now. I know you like children and animals so I hope you enjoy this one. I hear you said my name a few days ago, that is very special. I know you love us and I love you. I think of you very often and I took a picture of some old-fashioned woven beehives here in this former Yugoslavia. I will have it framed for you when I come home. There are a lot of beekeepers, or rather were a lot here, and I often think fondly of the times you and I enjoyed taking honey. As well I always think of the time you thought you could smell a bear and we could only find one slug. We were all concerned that the bear would destroy the hives then Leigh said he found the bear. It was his socks – ha, ha. And I remember how you hated the sapsuckers and Glenn said there was a duck in a tree and it was a sapsucker. So much for Glenn's bird recognition! Yes, I remember fondly all the times we had and wish we could talk about them. I will be home in April or May and I will come to visit with you and the nice ladies of the hospital who are so good to you. I know you think they are cute eh? Hands to yourself, buddy!

Things are tense here and could get worse. We are in a difficult position as UN troops, for, if we were not restricted we could kick some ass and settle it. But as it stands, I use my training to save lives of people who will never know they stepped in a spot where a mine once lay. I've run out of space so I will mail this to you and hopefully the next time you hear from me, I can hold your hand.

All my love, Your devoted grandson M.

During the Second World War, Arilius had been a school teacher and principal in rural Manitoba, teaching several young boys who would go on to serve in WWII. He would correspond with a few of these soldiers, becoming their pen pal, sending news and updates, lifting their spirits with familiarities of home. Well known in the community as a poet and wordsmith, he also served as the editor of *The Icelandic Canadian Magazine* for 26 years.

It is fitting to let his words speak now, to let his poetry and prose reveal the kind of person and role model that would inspire Mark to make a difference in the world. Arilius wrote this poem in June 1944. Coincidentally, it was fifty years to the month when his grandson was killed in the service of peace.

Graduation

Oh let me rise beyond my dreams,
Let me succeed in all that seems
So precious to my humble heart.
Give me courage to play my part

To shape the world where one can dwell
In peace and love, and refuse to sell
His soul to envy, hate and greed;
The sins that are the poisoned seed

Whose growth is like a running sore
And culminates a scab of war.
O help me to right the wrongs that are,
And from my thoughts all vision bar

Of selfish hopes, unworthy plans,
Of earthly schemes that are all man's.
Help me along the road of life,
A twisted path of toil and strife,

Where roses bloom with thorns unseen,
Teach me the sacrifice that's been
Displayed by those that went before
To make my task a lesser chore.

Give me strength to fight the blast
Of temptation's squalls and gales so vast.
Help me my faults to overcome
So at the end there may be some

Deed or act or thought or letter
I leave behind, mankind to better.

Two years after the close of the Second World War, haunting memories of destruction and loss, still fresh, Arilius asks the daunting question,

Is The Battle O'er?

Is the battle o'er when the warrior
Lays down his sword and gun?
Does the struggle last on down past
Where the foe break rank and run?
Does the treaty signed all strife there bind
And leave undone no task?

Not a life to live, but a life to give
To better the bread of all,
Not a love to spare, but a love to share
To turn to sweet the gall,

These are the acts wherein dwell the facts
Of prime pure peace on earth.
These are your duties of life's beauties
To give the world a great new birth.

'Till right has won, and wrong has gone
From every human heart,
'Till brotherhood is the heart's food
And soothes all hatred's smart,

There'll be no rest, but is a jest.
Does peace betray herself?
The battles won when every one

Is master of themselves.

G.B.A.Isfeld June 7, 1947

82

In an article written in 1967 for Canada's Centennial year, during a time of growth and prosperity unprecedented in Canadian history, Arilius predicts a new citizenry with global responsibilities.

Lastly, but quickly becoming the most significant, a good citizen considers himself a member of the world community. The idea that one's duties are to his nation only has been blotted out permanently as the speed of modern transportation and communication has made next door neighbours of nations to the ends of the world. As a member of the world community a good citizen respects all races and creeds irrespective of apparent differences. He carefully keeps in mind that what other nations are striving for is the direct result of their cultures and beliefs; that they are as sincere in their adherence to their way of life as he is in his.

He tries to understand their problems and thus recognize their viewpoints and accepts them without personally opinionated prejudice. This in turn means that a good citizen acquaints himself fully with world organizations and the part his own country plays in them. To the best of his ability he assists his own nation to be a member in good standing, always fostering better relations in order that peace, goodwill and due respect may be the result.

No longer is one able to give his whole loyalty to home and country; loyalty to the human race must have its share. The need of world citizenship has glaringly been thrust upon us. Let us hope that we can ably cope with it. May our centennial enthusiasm carry us forward, toward world citizenship.

Gudmundur Bjorjvin Arilius Isfeld 1967

Arilius lived out his last months in an extended care home, slowly succumbing to Alzheimer's grasp. His family and friends maintained a constant vigil. The sudden shock of Mark's death understandably had the family reeling, and Carol and Brian had responsibilities that needed their attention.

Dave and Lynn Breese attended Mark's funeral in Chilliwack then returned to Comox to Arilius' bedside. Together, with trusted staff members, they did what they had to do and told Arilius of Mark's death, the memorial service, and that Carol and Brian would return to him soon.

Brian journaled the last days of his dad's life, with friends and family present for the last good byes:

"Dad was labouring and seemingly still fighting the "Angel of Mercy" so close by him. He opened his eyes for about 30 seconds and looked at me but I don't really know if he recognized me at this time. Carol came down later and he immediately grasped her hand with a definite firmness different than the response to my male hand.

I went home and got my mother and father's wedding picture and picked a flower on the way in to the room. About twenty minutes later he opened his eyes wide. I took that opportunity to show him the picture, then I showed him the flower and moved it back and forth in front of him and there was definite eye movement following the flower. He closed his eyes and shortly thereafter died peacefully in the presence of Carol and I, and Dave and Lynn, Dave's wife."

Arilius Isfeld, born Dec 20, 1913, passed away June 29, 1994. There was an unspoken understanding in the room on the day that Arilius died. He had left as Brian described, "hand in hand to a better place with grandson Mark."

Who can predict whether Mark Isfeld would have carried out his life's path had he never known the passions and love of his grandparents? Mark grew up with his own innate characteristics for sure — but it is undeniable that his paternal grandparents Arilius and Steinunn, as well as his maternal grandparents George and Olina Donaldson, contributed to the shaping of Mark's conscience and moral fibre and to his life's role as a peacekeeper.

The mature love of a grandparent can reach past and above the instinctive fears of parents. It is a special influence that can leave an indelible mark on a child. It speaks in a continuous succession of teaching and learning moments that can profoundly affect the values and beliefs of the next generation. Parents and grandparents were key to the phenomenon of the Izzy Doll. The knitters, crocheters, volunteers who package, pick up and deliver — all contribute in their own way to lessen suffering and to bring hope.

Their actions resonate loud and clear that they "are in the mood for peace" and are in accord with Arilius' philosophy, particularly the last stanza of Graduation:

Help me my faults to overcome
So at the end there may be some
Deed or act or thought or letter
leave behind, mankind to better.

"He shouldn't have had to die because mines are insidious and should not exist. But I know that if Mark were alive he'd do it again because he had a great feeling for the elderly and the very young and the helpless."
A statement from Brian that appeared inSowing the Dragon's Teeth: Land Mines and the Global Legacy of War by Philip C. Winslow

At the time of Mark's death in 1994, the Internet was not yet a household word. As it was with anything that interested Brian, he utilized this emerging tool and learned its secrets. Using basic web-page code he built a memorial site about Mark. (Over the years, Brian acquired quite an impressive email list ranging from fellow hobbyists and other veterans to senators and generals.)

After the ritual of Mark's burial, and once the stream of relatives and visitors had ceased, the Isfelds found themselves alone with their grief. Brian reached out to an online compassionate group on the Internet. He etched out his pain in an essay-style letter which he said he had hoped would help someone else going through the same kind of hell as his family experienced. About his emotional pain-ride Brian wrote, "Tears do not readily flow. Anger dwells deep inside, occasionally coming irrationally to the fore, only to be quickly suppressed." He offered a logical rebuttal to the remarks thrown at him as a father of a soldier and suggested how to deal with a grieving person:

"Do not try to justify the passing of a person's loved ones with statements such as 'That's awful, but he knew what he was getting into when he took up the profession.' No profession one elects to follow has the foregone conclusion that one is going to die carrying it out. Say simply, and with sincerity, 'I'm sorry.' Period. On the other hand, do not avoid talking about the situation and circumstances when someone in grief broaches the subject."

He admitted that he had felt an almost fanatical desire to have people see and hear about Mark. He made presentations of plaques and donated a handcrafted trophy of Macassar ebony to be awarded to the most deserving member of his son's regiment. There were other gestures as well, but what Brian came to understand was that his actions were not just about memorializing his son. He wanted, even needed, responses and acknowledgments which were, "a confirmation that people do care and are concerned" and that he was not alone in his grief.

As the loss of a loved one often does, Mark's death challenged his father's philosophical beliefs about mortality and purpose. Brian prompted the readers of his essay to make their short time on this earth; "…a time in which we have the opportunity to give to the world an idea, an invention, a deed, a word, or a service that can be a legacy to those in the future. Our death need not be meaningless. Our deaths can be the vehicle for change for the better … I feel that Mark's death, and his deeds in life, can and will be an inspiration to make changes for the better of our country, and for all mankind in some way."

These were prophetic words and, as it turned out, they epitomized the work Brian pursued while working to ban landmines and help landmine survivors. Helping to free people from the bonds of landmines was something his son had believed in and died for.

"I addressed clearly the deficiencies in government and military support of those people left to carry on the peacekeeping job, directing my anger and frustration towards the politicians and hierarchy of the military in my country. I wrote many letters to media and political sources addressing my concerns to them."

Brian was publicly critical of the fact that trained canines were not utilized to sniff mines, something he called "common sense."

"It is not my intention to lay blame with the military or with anyone involved at the scene. I make here one, and only one, observation. Had they had at their disposal on the 21 June 1994 at the site where Mark was killed, dogs trained in explosives detection, my son would be alive today, I believe most emphatically."

An invitation was extended to Brian to offer his unique perspective as the grieving father of a Canadian soldier. It resulted in his words being heard and added to resource material for students studying Peacekeeping.

"I had the opportunity of being casually asked to visit a university in the United States to present my story if I was 'ever down that way.' This was a result of them using some of my material on the internet in a class being taught on peacekeeping. This casual invitation ultimately resulted in my wife and myself flying from the West Coast of Canada to Washington DC, and addressing the class at the university, and also the United States Institute of Peace."

Brian and Carol joined the Canadian Landmine Foundation and Brian became the Canadian representative for the Landmine Survivors Network. At an Ottawa convention for the banning of landmines he made his case for the survivors of landmines:

"By my own loose definition a victim is one who has for example been killed directly by a landmine, or lost the will to live, or lost the breadwinner of the family, and having no hope of help from any quarter, slowly perishes as surely as the victim who is killed outright.

The survivor, on the other hand, may be someone injured directly by a landmine; injured emotionally, such as family members or members of a group that must carry on with the tasks that injured or killed their comrade. Our Peacekeepers for example. They may have lost limbs, loved ones, or breadwinners, but if they receive support, encouragement, and concrete help they will survive. Our goal must be to ensure all who have had an encounter with a landmine and lived become survivors, not victims."

An evangelist for the real world as he saw it, Brian was known for handing out books with an authoritarian "read this" rather than continue to debate with someone he perceived as an uninformed participant. One such book was *All Quiet on the Western Front* written by a German veteran of the First World War trenches, Erich M. Remarque. He wrote of how difficult it was for soldiers to resume their life as they knew it after armistice, and how many who had escaped the physical wounds were emotionally or mentally destroyed by war. It accomplished Brian's mission to dispel any stereotype of the non-emotive, robotic soldier, and it raised awareness about the existence of post-traumatic stress and the toll it has taken throughout history. He forwarded emails, attachments and web sites towards the cause of enlightening me and on one visit he handed me a paperback accompanied by his customary authoritarian, "read this."

The book was *Canadian Peacekeepers* by N.S. Leach; it featured Mark's story and also the role of other Canadian soldiers deployed in UN Missions. I read of the standoff in the Medak Pocket, where rules of engagement constrained our soldiers while brutal torture and death to civilians ensued. Brian was proud of our soldiers for holding their ground and ultimately ending it in a truce, but he also spoke of the frustration with the political reality that soldiers are forced to endure and that ties the hands.

I read about General Dallaire's chilling revelation and his thwarted efforts to save 800,000 Rwandans from genocide. A compassionate soul-searching soldier, Dallaire witnessed and was powerless to halt, the "unimaginable carnage" as his requests for supplementary troops to curb the rising numbers of deaths were refused. He subsequently returned home emotionally injured and faced his own personal war with PTSD. It was Brian and Carol's opinion that General Dallaire was a true Canadian hero.

Brian was sincere in his attempts to lead people to the 'truth' of the noble and humanitarian side of our soldiers. He pointed out that soldiers are mere humans who must stand up to, or are caught up in, a pervading and destructive force that has been part of our world — and perhaps our makeup — since time began. He forwarded one of his favourite quotes about soldiering that succinctly summed it up; "It's no job for a soldier but only a soldier can do it."

***

The Izzy Doll project bridged Brian's logical world with Carol's emotional one. It began as a resolution to carry on their son's legacy, but Brian found a new role working alongside his wife. He posted the Izzy Doll pattern on Mark's memorial website and Carol relied on his Internet savvy to send messages and updates. When Carol expressed a fear of a child or soldier killed while giving out dolls, Brian went right to the top.

"I talked to General Hillier the Chief of the defence staff at Rideau Hall. I told him about my reticence about sending dolls to Afghanistan and having a headline show up about some poor guy getting killed handing a doll to a kid. He said no way. The dolls are great icebreakers for the troops when they go into negotiations, and the guys are going to interact with the kids anyway so it might as well be dolls as candy and other stuff."

In fact there were times when the distribution of dolls was halted for cautionary reasons. Knowing that our soldiers would not be in any unnecessary danger due to the gift giving was a relief to Carol.

Brian helped package and mail and performed other duties to see the Izzy Doll project continue to grow. Pat said that the Izzy Dolls brought her brother and his wife closer together. "They worked as a team and he supported her with the dolls."

Our nation saw it, too, and Carol and Brian were jointly awarded the Meritorious Service Medal (civil division). Brian had related that when Carol began making the dolls, Mark had been hopeful it could help his mother focus her energy on something positive rather than worry about him. He would have been pleased to see his folks not only working together but being awarded national recognition for their joint efforts.

Archived on the Government of Canada's web site the citation reads:

"Brian Lynthor Isfeld, M.S.M., C.D., Courtenay, British Columbia
Carol Margaret Isfeld, M.S.M., Courtenay, British Columbia
Meritorious Service Medal

In 1994, Brian and Carol Isfeld's son, MCpl Mark Isfeld, was killed in Croatia while carrying out UN peacekeeping duties. To honour their son's memory, the Isfelds continue to this day to craft, ship and promote the delivery of the nicknamed 'Izzy' dolls to Canadian soldiers. They, in turn, give them to orphaned and vulnerable children in war-torn regions around the world.

Through their generosity and compassion, Mr. and Mrs. Isfeld have kept this tradition alive while alleviating the suffering of children."

Brian was proud when recognition came to his wife in 2000 with the invitation to represent mothers of our fallen at the National Remembrance Day Ceremony in Ottawa. The Isfelds attended and Carol played a prominent role. Brian watched from the sidelines as she placed the wreath the morning of November 11. He listened to the speeches and all the while an uneasy gnawing in the pit of his gut was sending an unsettling message.

He had gone through the motions standing solemnly alongside 15,000 people amassed during this formal, nationally televised ceremony. It was a sincere effort to pay tribute and remember our veterans and our fallen. A sincere attempt, yet not enough to satisfy the father of a soldier killed in the service of his country. The inner dialogue of a father's logic reasoned that a one-day remembrance service wasn't adequate to "keep alive the acts of heroism and sacrifice of my son and the sons and daughters of countless others in past conflicts… I have to do something, albeit I do not, for the life of me know what, to rectify this situation, to cry out loudly that we must always remember, not just today and I think what the Hell, nobody who is not directly involved really gives a damn."

His anger and frustration would be allayed, and his questions answered the next morning, in a most unexpected manner.

REMEMBRANCE

In canada we have a tendancy to go out of our way to bury our heroes and their memory, they (other nations) just bury the hero.

Brian Isfeld

The most important part of this trip to Ottawa, in Brian's estimation, played out at the cenotaph on November 12, the morning after Remembrance Day. It unfolded in a modern setting, yet it was a scene that Charles Dickens could very well have written, with Brian as the main character. Before leaving Ottawa, Brian wanted to take the last few pictures on his roll of film. He was still carrying the anger from the previous day's memorial service, convinced that it would be another year before most people would care about this place. The hands of an intervening force waited patiently for the opportunity to change his "cynical view of humanity and remembrance."

Low and behold…

Tomb of the Unknown Soldier

Ottawa Cenotaph

"I was sitting by the Tomb of the Unknown Soldier, watching two teenage boys, undoubtedly the scourge of all us over 50 years old, as they skateboarded along the now not so busy roads encircling the cenotaph. I could see they were preparing to cross the grounds from one side to another, and I thought to myself, "Could they not find some other flat expanse of concrete to skate on? Did they have to play on this area that was just yesterday blessed with Veterans and onlookers in Remembrance?

To my amazement they stopped short at the very point that the red carpet had been just yesterday, the very point where Carol and others had walked the carpet to lay the wreaths of Remembrance, and there they each picked up their skateboard, and proceeded to walk, and walk solemnly I might add - glancing briefly and respectfully at the Tomb of the Unknown Soldier, across the concrete until they reached the other side where they placed their boards down and noisily resumed skating the streets. This from two young devil-may-care boys, their ball-caps turned incongruously backwards on their heads, their baggy pants making one wonder they could walk, let alone skate the board without getting all tangled up in a heap. A twinge of hope permeated me briefly."

This first missive generated a spark of optimism, but it was insufficient to erode layers and years of scepticism. His mental toughness served him well during his military career and he would not be easily shifted from his beliefs. A man prone to logic and the rational, he would be harder to convince. Good thing a divine dispatch comes in threes. "Immediately after this phenomenon, while I was still in semi shock at what I had just witnessed, a jogger, hell bent for election, came streaking across the cement. The cynicism of my mind abruptly kicked in, and I thought to myself, "Hey you, old enough to know better. Could you not find some place better suited to your morning jog than this sacred place? No sooner had the thought formed in my mind than this jogger, having arrived directly in front of the Tomb of the Unknown Soldier, stopped as if having been shot. He turned to the tomb and replete in sweat suit and sweater, with toque covering his ears and almost his eyes, he saluted the Tomb and turned to continue his jog, disappearing on the other side of the cenotaph where the teenage boys had gone! This whole episode took perhaps two seconds, yet it seemed to me to encompass time enough for a whole ceremonial event. And indeed it was a ceremonial event."

Walking across to the cenotaph, Brian's eyes fell on a long-stemmed, crimson rose lying naked on the barren cement. Eerily reminiscent of the red roses their family had draped over his son's casket six years earlier, this would be the third and final missive for today. Left by an unknown 'stranger' and signed with a single familiar letter, Brian knew with surety it was a message for him and a message for us all. "Continuing my way around, I spied on the cold, hard granite of the steps surrounding the cenotaph, a rose that I thought someone had missed when picking up the wreaths and objects of remembrance that had been laid. I had three pictures left in my camera and decided that this was about as good a picture as any. I stepped over to the rose and noticed a card lying under the single stem of the deep-blood-red flower. I read the card, then took the pictures as tears welled up in my eyes, knowing that what I was reading and experiencing this morning was what it was all about. The card read:

IN LOVING MEMORY Nov 2000

Dear Poppa,
I miss you today more than these words can say.
We are here now as a family and as a country
because of your love for us, because of your courage,
I will never forget what you did for us.
I Love You.

M. xoxoxox

The signature, a single initial M, was how Mark often signed his letters home. Chills ran down the back of Brian's neck; he was now consciously aware of the possibility that Mark's hand was at work, partnering with the divine to bring peace to his father's agitated heart. Brian would never know the name of the soldier the card was actually intended for, only that he was destined to find it.

Three messages delivered and accepted buoyed his confidence. He now knew that many Canadians, of all ages and from all walks of life, would remain loyal to the memory of the soldiers and all they had sacrificed. "I no longer feel despair, and I no longer feel anger. I am still greatly saddened at the loss of our son, and sad at the loss of our citizenry from past wars, but I am overjoyed having experienced this morning, knowing in my heart that if the actions of individuals I witnessed this morning are any indicator, the memories and respect shown by these three incidents ensure that remembrance will be strong, sincere, and meaningful in the future." Three days after returning from their trip to Ottawa, Brian recorded the account of November 11th and 12th on Mark's memorial page. His lone experience at the Ottawa Cenotaph, he hoped, would hearten other parents and families who needed to know their loved ones would never be forgotten.

Author's note: On November 11, 2005, which was celebrated as The Year of the Veteran, a Seventh Book of Remembrance was dedicated by the Governor General. This book was initiated by RCAF pilot (retired) Syd Burrows. It was a heartfelt quest to ensure all of those killed in the service during 'peace time' would also be duly remembered. Syd said, "More than 1600 have died ... Cold War, NORAD, United Nations, NATO (including Afghanistan-Europe), Training, and SAR operations." Two hundred of those were Syd's friends and comrades. Syd had initiated a working group, a committee made up of what he called 'exceptional people' who worked closely with their MPs, Veterans Affairs Advisory Committee and talented artisans. Syd and Brian Isfeld had never met but ironically they lived near each other in the twin cities of Comox and Courtney B.C.

According to Veterans' Affairs website, at the unveiling, Canada's Silver Cross mother, Claire Léger mother of Sergeant Marc Léger, 3rd Battalion, PPCLI, killed in Afghanistan in 2002, said, "Our son, and all the others who died may not have been in wars, but they died for their country... I'm totally thrilled to have his name inscribed in a book forever; I'm so appreciative of the work that's gone into the book. It's amazing."

Mark Isfeld's name is also included in this book. The Seventh Book of Remembrance resides with the other Six Books of Remembrance in the Memorial Chapel in the Peace Tower, Ottawa.

PROJECT H.O.P.E

"The demons aren't gone. The point of continuing therapy is to learn how to beat them, how to respond when they rear up in response to a smell, a sound, some trigger of the past." Learning this control, Stephane discovered, makes it possible to get back on track."

An excerpt from Stephane Grenier's story
Peer Support Testimony, www.osiss.ca

Lt.-Col. Stephane Grenier had served under General Dallaire in Rwanda in what was historically labelled "one of the most horrific events of the 20th Century." He returned injured but not from a bullet wound or the loss of a limb, which would be readily understood as an injury and gain empathy from the military and Canadians. He returned wounded with an operational stress injury (OSI), a phrase he coined while studying the ambiguous creature that sought to destroy his life. PTSD is any past event(s) traumatically impacting on the mind; OSI is a similar psychological injury suffered by soldiers deployed in the service of their country.

In an article on OSI Grenier states, "Those who suffer from OSI have had their image of fairness or stability of the world so disrupted that they are forced to devote much of their time and energy adjusting to the emotional disturbance this has caused." Soldiers witnessing moral and ethical dilemmas and who feel a powerlessness to circumvent a tragic outcome are vulnerable to OSI. Symptoms present themselves in the form of substance abuse, agitation, violent outbursts, suicide, insomnia, relationship problems, personality changes and more. A smell or sound can trigger a fierce reaction instantly transporting a soldier back in time and place to the upheaval that caused his invisible wounds. The negative stigma and judgments surrounding stress injuries compounds the problem, and soldiers who do not know help is available can isolate themselves and withdraw from the world.

Stephane Grenier, project director for The Operational Stress Injury Social Support project (OSISS), which started in 2001, was convinced that the unconditional understanding offered by someone who has been through an OSI could help a soldier to heal. Therefore, peer support was the foundation of the OSISS program.

Once OSISS was available and working for soldiers, Marley Leger, the wife of Sgt. Marc Leger who was killed by friendly fire at the Tarnak Farm incident, approached Grenier and asked what was available for grieving families of soldiers killed on duty. As a result, a planning group of seven widows and two fathers was launched under the umbrella of OSISS.

***

Brian may have seemed like an unlikely candidate to join a compassionate outreach group but he had had first-hand knowledge of the power of peer support and its effectiveness to heal. Although it was not a subject he brought up often, Brian had been a member of Alcoholics Anonymous since his sons were boys. There is an unwritten belief that soldiers who drink together form a cohesive bond, but as a young father Brian's belief in that began to erode. After more than a decade in the service he made the decision to quit drinking.

His sister explains; "He never lost a day of work, but drinking wasn't doing anything for him as a husband, a father or the military. You need to know when you need help. The roots of his ability to counsel and understand people's reticence to accept help came from the experience of working within AA."

Word of the inception of a peer support group fell on Brian's ears and he signed up. Soon after, a reporter asked Brian a question that he now had an answer for: "What did the military ever do for you when your son died?" Brian notified the reporter of the meeting on May 31, 2006, in Edmonton, that could potentially be the beginning of a family support program and which was a very long time in coming.

"We walk in this valley together. We are not alone."
Jim Davis, father of Cpl Paul Davis
killed in Afghanistan March 2, 2006

The flurry of media outside Jim and Sharon Davis' front door signified a nightmare of a day that could never be erased. Military protocol, when a soldier is killed, is to deliver the news to the next of kin, usually the wife. Jim and Sharon's daughter-in-law, Melanie, had called them that pivotal morning with the sickening news that Paul had been killed and seven others injured. Jim Davis held his wife in his arms as the pall of sorrow settled in around them. It was hard to breathe or even think straight. Stunned by the news, Jim says he was oblivious to his surroundings, even to the reporters gathering outside his front door. He wanted to tell the world what a great son Paul was but didn't make the connection to the opportunity out on the sidewalk until his 12-year-old son, Craig, pointed it out.

A friend had offered to send the reporters away when Craig, who was witnessing the emotional turmoil in the room and the commotion on the street, proved to be the voice of reason, saying, "But Dad, a few minutes ago you said you wanted to tell the whole world about Paul. Now's your chance."

For Jim, it was an overwhelming inner struggle to make sense of what happened, to be consoled somehow so he could be strong for his family. The phone rang. A father who had lost his son in Afghanistan the previous November was on the other end of the line. Jim says he will never forget the powerful words of Dan Woodfield. "Mr. Davis, you are now where I was three months ago." Jim wondered how a stranger who was just as devastated as he was could pick up the phone and offer some comfort. It was a remarkable gift of generosity that Jim much later called, "a single act that gave me real comfort and hope." Jim said that Mr. Woodfield's phone call was the first indication that he was not alone.

Over the next few days a steady flow of people reached out and offered their condolences and prayers. But everything seemed so inadequate to fill the crater that Paul's death had left. Another unexpected knock at the door meant yet another well-intentioned person had arrived. Father Michael Walsh, a neighbour from down the street, stepped inside. Jim poured a brew of coffee and served up a personal spiritual query, one I'm sure Father Walsh had heard from other grieving Christians when unexplainable tragedy befalls them.

Father Michael listened to Jim's outpourings. "Michael, all I want is for Jesus to come through that front door and with His arms open embrace me, comfort me, and tell me that Paul was with Him. But, Michael, I am a realist and know that that is impossible. He is not going to come through that door. God does not work that way."

Father Walsh replied, "But, Jim, I do see Jesus coming through your front door. I have seen him every day since Paul was killed. He comes in the form of each and every person who comes bringing their condolences."

In that moment a flood of faces of those who had reached out to him and his family rolled through his mind as if they were a cast of characters on a movie screen. There was Mr. Woodfield who had the courage to call Jim on the day Paul died, and the visitors, friends and neighbours who brought food, cards, and flowers or had sent emails. And there was another significant phone call with a message so timely it was as though Paul had engineered it himself.

Jim had been questioning whether Paul knew how much he had loved him and "whether Paul loved me." Then a telephone call came from someone Paul had spoken so highly of from his past but who his dad had never met. Jim trusted the words of this stranger. In his youth Paul had spent a year with his biological mother living in Ontario, far away from his dad. He had bonded with another teenager who had taught him to play hockey, at which Paul had excelled. Paul had left an indelible mark on that young man, now grown. He had taken the time to call Jim to say, "When he left it was like I lost a brother. I want you to know Paul loved you very much. All he ever talked about was you."

Father Walsh's words brought solace and an epiphany for Jim that Jim talks about to this day, "Jesus comes to me through everyone. It's that simple. It is right, and if that's the way God works, I'll allow it."

Jim did heed the advice of young Craig and took the opportunity to tell Paul's story. He spoke of how throughout Paul's life he had stood up to the bullies to protect the underdog. He said Paul's pursuit of adventure motivated him to join the military just out of high school. Because of Paul's loyalty and duty toward his comrades he turned down a promotion that would have seen him avoid service in Afghanistan. Jim told of how Paul had a strong sense of purpose to free the women and children of Afghanistan, victims of the Taliban rule and bullies in Paul's mind.

He talked about their last walk together in the snow just outside the air terminal before Paul's departure. The reality of deployment to Afghanistan was evident in his soldier son's voice. He questioned whether God was real and then questioned if he was capable of killing another human being. Jim said he could see it was a moral issue that worried his son. Paul outlined the arrangements he had made for his wife Melanie and their two daughters should something happen; necessary details that soldiers must face.

Jim made a promise to look out for the girls and hugged his son. They said their good-byes for the last time and Paul boarded his plane.

***

The path Jim Davis chose to take after his son's death was influenced by the compassion others had shown during his family's darkest days. Today he talks about the experiences saying they have made him feel stronger and more alive. He has made new friends he would never have known if he had withdrawn into a protective cocoon. "Father Michael's words had encouraged me to accept these new encounters with open arms. I could have chosen to carry on and bury myself in my work but I didn't. My life wouldn't have been as rich."

It was a reporter who called Jim to inform him of the initial planning meeting for a family bereavement support group in Edmonton. Jim called the invitation he received a week later mysterious, but a shining light of hope he knew he had to accept. He said he felt compelled to "reach out and embrace other loved ones of fallen soldiers." He said he knew what he had to do. He went.

> But wait, look back, someone is standing there.
> They are alone and want to cross the stepping stones.
> I'd better go. They need my help.
> What? Are you sure? Why, yes, go ahead. I'll wait.
> You know the way. You've been there.
> Yes, I agree. It's your turn, my friend...
> To help someone else cross the stepping stones.

An excerpt from Barbara Williams' poem
Together We Walk the Stepping Stones

A bereavement peer helper group emerged from that first meeting in Edmonton attended by a group of nine; seven women and two men; Brian and Jim. The members chose the acronym H.O.P.E. meaning Helping Others by Providing Empathy, to define their network of compassion. Sophie Richard, the Assistant Program Manager of H.O.P.E., said it was a privilege to lead this "wonderful group."

Meeting for the first time was an experience that Jim Davis admits was "more powerful and intense than any conference, meeting or workshop I had ever attended; and more satisfying and fulfilling."

I'm sure Jim captures Brian's sentiments, too, as he explains what it was like to tell his story within the safety of H.O.P.E. "I could see that others in the room could feel my pain. They got it. They knew exactly what I was feeling and as they told their stories I felt the loneliness, the pain, the fear and the guilt that these widows were feeling. I felt it and I cared."

Listening to the widows' stories no doubt gave Jim and Brian a deeper perspective of the feelings of a grieving woman, whether she was a wife or a mother. "To hear what they felt was exactly how I felt." And even more. Jim elaborated, "What my daughter-in law was going through, losing her friend, companion, lover, breadwinner and a parent of their children. And hearing how a wife copes if their children look like their father and they have to look into their eyes daily — and be reminded."

There were other sessions over the months, and one particularly emotional day that solidified Jim's focus and united the two fathers. All nine members were sitting together when it was reported that four more soldiers had fallen. It hit Jim hard. "Emotion came over me as though I just heard Paul was killed."

Jim was the newest one to the grief process, and when he felt the need to leave the room to gain his composure Brian followed. "I'm outside having a cigarette when Brian comes out and stands next to me. Brian's got a cigarette lit. I ask him, 'Brian, it has been over twelve years for you, does it ever get any better?' He looked up at the clouds and sky and inhaled deep. 'Nope.'

I had to learn to live with this and deal with it.' I said 'Let's go back in.'"

Jim says of that day, "I knew I had to find a way to live with this pain, this pain that will always be with me. The answer to how to live with it was right there, back in that room where my peers were waiting. I was going to help myself by helping others." He understood that was what Brian was doing also.

It was true that H.O.P.E. meetings could be emotionally intense but Jim clarified that not only did they share boxes of tissues, they also laughed together and teased each other. It felt good to laugh. He described Brian as a "rascal" acting like he was a plucky schoolboy again.

"He was hard of hearing and he would play it up saying, 'Whaaa' can you speak up, I'm hard of hearing!'"

Brian once challenged a professional who presented at a workshop on grieving by saying, "Excuse me I thought you said we all have to be in a circle. Why are you sitting at the desk?" Although it may have been tongue in cheek, Brian did have a history for holding people to task, and the higher their position the more he expected.

Sophie agreed that Brian had contributed significantly to their group. "Brian was, in my eyes, a giver with so many gifts to offer. Our relationship had a lot of humour, and sometimes I must say some controlling issues. The bereavement peer-helper group had many laughs with Brian. The one that comes to mind was during their training in Ottawa. Brian had the habit of leaving his teeth in his pocket, well, on the Wednesday Brian lost his teeth. We looked everywhere, the conference room, called the taxi company, etc. No luck. Finally they went back to the hotel. The receptionist handed Brian a plastic baggie with his teeth safely inside."

Jim continued the story, "Brian sent me to the bar to buy a triple scotch. (I'd never seen him drink — Scotch is expensive and I had no clue as to why he wanted it.). When I passed him the glass I was shocked and speechless as he dropped his teeth into it. And, of course, he gave that little giggle of his."

Brian always had a good joke followed by his characteristic sly grin, but when it came to his role as a peer support volunteer he took it very seriously. Sophie says of his contribution: "Brian's role in OSISS was a provider of hope and comfort for those who, like him, lost a family member. By his generous, sincere and compassionate approach he was able to make such a profound difference in the lives of those who were suffering. Each time I would ask Brian if he could reach out to another family his answer was always the same, 'Yes Sophie let's do it.'"

Monsters in the Dark
I know that they are out there: I will not be ignorant anymore:
Pulling the blanket over my head will not keep them from coming ashore;
Instead I choose to confront them as afraid as I might be;
Because if I don't stop the monsters our children can never be free.

Written by MCpl Jeffrey Walsh in 2006 to explain to his three young children why he was returning to Afghanistan

Front Row: Ben and Margie Walsh, Padre Monpas, Brian, Scott Fairweather Back Row: Paul Faucette

Ben Walsh is jolly and looks good in red. A retired RCMP officer, he could appreciate his son's chosen career path just as his son, Jeffrey, understood the role of his father's work to protect and uphold the peace. Margie Walsh has gentle eyes and is petite and soft-spoken. Margie and Ben have two children. Jeffrey was their only son. When Jeffrey was killed in Afghanistan in 2006 Jeff's parents were on Brian's radar to contact and lend his support.

Jeffrey was a highly proficient soldier who believed he was making a difference. In an *Ottawa Citizen* interview prior to his deployment he commented, "We are over there to bring stability to a nation that doesn't have it." Margie said it was difficult for Jeffrey to talk about his first tour of duty in Afghanistan, but one day he opened up. In a radio interview with CBC Radio's *The Current* she described how he had talked briefly about the disparity between the abundance in Canada and those in jeopardy in Afghanistan who had nothing but the clothes on their back. He mirrored what Mark Isfeld had pointed out over a decade before; that we just don't know how well off we are in Canada.

Just days after returning to Kandahar, Master Corporal Jeffrey Walsh lost his life in a weapons related accident. A young man of 33, he left his wife Julie, their three children, a sister and his mother and father.

Ben, Jeffrey and Margie

Linda Loree, mother of Nathan Horneburg killed in Afghanistan September 24, 2007

Ben and Margie were numb at the future without Jeffrey. Then Brian's phone call came, as Ben said, "out of the blue." It was the beginning of several conversations per week, and ongoing for more than a year. He also said it was a phone call that had made a difference.

As he thought back to their conversations Ben smiled and said, "Brian would always begin his calls the same way. 'Do you have your coffee yet?' and 'What are you going to do today?'

A common reaction to grief is to pull away from the world and turn inward, which can easily lead to depression. Brian's well-directed questions helped Ben focus on a plan for the day that would distract him from the pitfall of despair. "Brian made me stop and think, and you need room for thoughts when you are grieving. He helped me on my journey; it's a long journey. I'd put a gold star on him."

Ben talked about how Brian handled topics smoothly, helped him to see another viewpoint and to take a different approach to handling a situation. The Walsh's were grateful for Brian's gift of his experience and the eminent message that resounded with them, "You are not alone." Ben summed it up, "People helping people; that's what it is. If the program didn't exist it wouldn't be good, wouldn't be good at all."

"The world is full of suffering; it is also full of overcoming it."

Helen Keller

H.O.P.E. is the solid ground beneath the unstable feet of the survivors of war — the families who, in the past, were forgotten. They were expected to reconstruct their lives by piecing together a family picture puzzle with missing, irreplaceable parts.

There had been nothing like a peer support network in place for families like the Isfelds or for the families throughout our nation's history. I have wondered whether Carol Isfeld would have suffered less and lived longer if the Program of H.O.P.E. or its equivalent had been available decades earlier. Even though the program was not founded until twelve years after Mark's death, H.O.P.E. gave Brian an avenue to heal and to grow by assisting others to manoeuvre around their emotional obstacles. I believe it made him a more compassionate man.

✳✳✳

The meeting of Jim Davis and Brian Isfeld had materialized because of a personal loss that drew them into the program of H.O.P.E. But it was many a good argument that had cemented their friendship. Not only did they come from opposite ends of our country, they were opposite personalities with different points of view. Jim was a Liberal, diplomatic and stately in appearance. Brian, more concerned with comfort than fashion, called a spade a spade and called himself a Conservative. About Brian's tenacity Jim says he was like a dog with a bone, "When Brian got a hold of something he wouldn't let go. He was frustrating and made me so angry at times. It was his way or none."

But both were intelligent men who had mastered the craft of public speaking and appeared to be exhilarated at the opportunity to verbally spar (or "debate" as they would say) with each other on current issues.

Brian respected Jim's opinion so much so that he would email his essays to Jim for final reading. And Jim admitted there were plenty of times when the 'rascal' was right. In 2007 Brian nagged his friend to attend the Peacekeepers weekend. Jim said he couldn't justify the cost of traveling from the Maritimes to Calgary. Brian kept at him. Finally, they were down to the final hour and the last straw. Brian confessed, "I didn't want to tell you but your son's name will be on the Wall of Honour in Peacekeepers Park."

About their relationship Jim says, "Ever since Paul's death I believe I receive gifts of life. These gifts come in the form of beautiful souls who enter my life. Brian was one of these people. I miss Brian because he was so level headed and helped me in the directions I was choosing."

About the Peacekeepers weekend in 2007 Jim added, "Some mysterious force took me to Calgary. That mysterious force was called Brian."

PEACEKEEPERS' WEEKEND 2007

"All The Fallen Must Be So Recognized."

Motto of Peacekeeper Park

Peacekeeper Park in Calgary's southwest is a legacy project established on former military land. It stands among fifty-year-old trees, lush perennials, a playground area for children, and walking paths that lead to the focal points of the park.

The Wall of Honour is a prominent feature with the names of our fallen Peacekeepers engraved into the rock face. Mark Isfeld's name is there. Beside this wall is another, listing the missions in which the soldiers were deployed when they were killed. Descriptive words that speak loud and proud about the purpose of their missions make an impression in more ways than one. Words like stabilization, reconstruction, development, peace restoration, peace support, treaty, cooperation, and humanitarian peacemaking, are constructive and action-oriented words. These are words that are not present on other war memorials I have seen.

A third monument stands in Peacekeeper Park. The whole concept of an Izzy Doll as a token of peace is exemplified by a life-size, bronze statue of a soldier giving a doll to a child. It is Mark's story, memorialized, and the Isfelds were there for that momentous dedication in August of 2004.

Three years later, Brian arrived in Calgary alone, his flight booked to return to Courtney on the following Tuesday. He had a list of people to meet, and deeds and errands, including collecting photos for Carol as he had promised. He would also visit the Military Museums to hand off a travel bag full of Izzy Dolls allocated for shipping and distribution and collect a family artefact that had been on loan as a museum exhibit.

Brian had settled into his room at the Carriage House Inn where he would meet up with more out-of-towners arriving for the weekend. I had volunteered as the 'taxi' and he had issued me my first task; to meet Jim Davis at the airport. "He'll be wearing a suit. He's a politician," he directed.

Dapper in his blue suit, jacket over his arm and towing his wheeled carry-on, Jim was easy to identify. A smile from ear to ear reminded me of someone I had seen recently — of course, it was his son Paul. Brian had sent me a photograph of him. There was quite a resemblance.

"Never, and I stress NEVER, in my 68 years have I met someone so earthly yet so confident in his faith in his God and his fellow man as 'Paul of the smoking prayer.' This can have nothing but a positive effect on me, and of course on all of us who were drawn together on that fateful and I stress fateful weekend.'

Excerpt from Brian's journal about the Peacekeepers' Weekend August 2007

Father Paul Monpas, whom we called the Padre, joined our group. For the rest of the weekend our entourage consisted of the four of us; the two debaters Brian and Jim in the back, and the Padre beside me in the passenger seat.

Father Monpas was a soft-spoken man, with a hypnotic voice and melodic words shaped by his French Canadian accent. Like Brian the Padre was a realist, sincere but called a spade a spade too. And like Brian he had a history of stepping up to oppose injustices through his actions. In fact, when there was no one to commit to a young boy who was in desperate need of a loving parent the Padre adopted him. He spoke of the great reward it had been to become a father and now a grandfather. Brian was duly impressed with the unorthodox path of this man of God who was profoundly affecting his viewpoint on religion and spirituality.

Although this weekend was a solemn occasion and each had reason to be withdrawn into their own reflection, I was struck by the men's spirit for life and their ease at finding joy in the moment. Each day as we drove to events at different locations we laughed together, got lost, and learned a little more about one another. Comments from the two debaters strapped in the backseat while a woman driver, who was a mere stranger, chauffeured them did not go unnoticed. It was reminiscent of my days taxiing my children to sports events. The rowdier boys in the back were laughing and joking and me asking, "Would you like to share what's so funny?"

The Padre served as our navigator. When we came to a crossroad he'd hold his cane toward the window as though witching for water and declare "This way." This was always followed by his hearty laughter, which had us all joining in. Surprisingly he was correct; we always arrived at our destinations on time.

I felt honoured to be standing with Brian, Jim and Father Monpas in Peacekeeper Park for the Sunday service. There was a feeling of community. Parents from across our country were standing together with friends and strangers for one purpose; to remember and pay tribute to our fallen Peacekeepers. Brian and I watched as Jim read his son's name on the Wall of Honour for the first time and touched the stone edifice where the letters were inscribed. I met Maureen Eykelenboom and Margie and Ben Walsh, whose stories had preceded them through Brian's emails.

Jim Davis at the Wall of Honour, Peacekeeper's Park, Calgary

Father Monpas, who modeled the love and compassion of God in his life, did so once again as he delivered prayers to the grieving families and fellow Canadians in attendance.

The Padre's demeanour and the surety of his convictions were evident. I felt drawn to ask if he would talk with a friend of mine who was not searching for answers but who had made up his mind. David, who played in our band, was raised in Ireland during Northern Ireland's troubled years. Episodes of religious hatred and war had affected the psyche of a nation, and it stained his childhood. He said he was not biased. He harboured a distain for all religions and all wars. He suspected that if hatred was the opposite of the love that religions professed, there was clearly something else going on.

Color Party at the Peacekeeper Ceremony

Padre Monpas invited David to join us for supper at Brian's favourite seafood restaurant. Conversation was light as we finished our main course. The Padre broke the ice and asked David where he grew up in Ireland. Their dialogue continued and David opened up about the killings and bombings between two religious groups that made no sense to him as a child and less sense as a grown man. He showed his inconsolable sadness for the victims of war and the frustration with man's inclination to exploit and manipulate in the name of power and under the guise of religion. He gave examples of the dogma that he believed had hurt the Irish and that hindered his country, not helped it. The abuse of power by those in positions of trust was reprehensible in David's opinion. That was a viewpoint we all shared.

As the Padre listened, genuinely interested, I was observing Brian, who was strangely quiet. A spicy discussion was being served on a plate before him and he sat with both arms crossed peering up through the space between his spectacles and brows, silent. It was as though David was his surrogate debater. He watched

Brian and David O' Toole

and waited for the Padre's response. The Padre made no excuses, nor argument. In fact he agreed with David saying there were people who should not be wearing the cloth, people in all walks of life who bring a bad name to their profession or vocation, and that it was only through the grace of God that we can find forgiveness. That was a truth we all agreed upon.

There was something about this man of God that connected with Brian. After the conversation wound down, Brian rose with the Padre for what Brian called a "smoking prayer" — a cigarette. The chat continued outside in the evening air. Something had engaged that night. Something we wouldn't understand until later that week.

The second significant meeting happened the next day during Jim's departure. With parking taken care of, we approached the airport doors as Jim checked his ticket again. We had arrived two hours earlier than the two hours needed for boarding. Brian thought that was amusing and advantageous for now he had the time to speak with Security about the artefact he wanted to take on board the plane on his flight the next day. Brian pulled out a small device from a plastic bag he had tucked under his arm and held it in his hands for full view. Somehow he had obtained the casing of the landmine that had killed his son. It seemed macabre to me and Jim, but not Brian. Our mouths hung open.

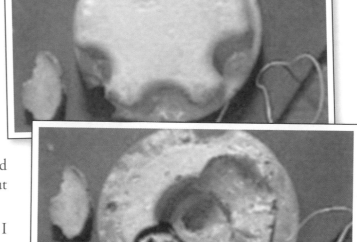

"They won't let you take that on the plane," I argued.

"Briiiaaan. Are you nuts?" Jim chided.

Maybe owning this broken contraption gave Brian a sense of power over it, or maybe he appreciated the shock value that was certainly guaranteed. Regardless, Brian wasn't deterred by our opposition and he grinned as he shuffled past us with his characteristic short-legged gait disappearing into the airport. But just minutes later he came back out, running and with excitement in his voice blurted out, "There are soldiers coming in from Afghanistan."

We hurried to Arrivals and reached the top of the escalator to the welcome signs, balloons, friends and family obviously excited about welcoming their returning soldiers. We were three flies on the wall positioned behind the small crowd, who were oblivious to us.

The two fathers stood silent. Not a word was exchanged. Minutes rolled by and Jim, who had been watching the door, sighed, "I can't do this."

Understanding the emotional jolt these dads were feeling, I offered to walk the adjacent hall with Jim.

A few more moments passed, "No." he said, determined to see it through, "I can do this." Brian was deep in thought, somewhere far away.

Then the automated doors opened and a soldier in Khakis with a great smile on his face walked through. We watched as his loved ones surrounded him with hugs and tears and laughter. The giant human welcoming ball moved as a unit down the stairs and into the August morning, a picture of reunion and elation. Brian and Jim were the testament to the other side of the same 'family' coin; the families who would never see their soldier again and whose grief would awaken and swell, subside and languish until the next memory or trigger.

We strolled through the adjacent hall and past a newsstand, where the soldier's return had made the headlines. The newspaper told of only one soldier, Jeff Taylor, returning on that Monday, August 13, 2007. Years later I asked Jim what he had been thinking while waiting for the doors to open that day. He verified what I had expected; that although he was truly elated for Jeff's family and his safe return, he wished his son Paul would walk through those doors too.

Jim's sentiment was likely what Brian felt too. These two men were as opposite as the Odd Couple, but they shared a history of loss and a pride they felt for our soldiers. Jim boarded his plane having admitted that Brian was right; this was a weekend he couldn't have missed.

I drove Brian to the airport the next day and said good-bye, but in Brian's inimitable way, there would be a series of good-byes yet to give before the final farewell.

Brian takes a photo of Jim Davis, Phyllis and
Padre Paul Alain Monpas at Peacekeeper Park, Calgary

THE UNEXPECTED

Good-byes are not forever. Good-byes are not the end. They simply mean I'll miss you, until we meet again!

Author Unknown

Daily calls to Carol had kept Brian aware of her condition, but when their neighbours contacted him to say she was in Emergency he realized the situation was serious. He was anxious to get home. Arriving Tuesday night directly from the airport, Brian wrote, "She was experiencing much pain at that time, but her spirits were high none the less." Carol was scheduled for surgery on Thursday to remove an intestinal blockage that was causing her unbearable pain. The uncertainty of it all was reminiscent of the emotional toll of losing Mark, and the Isfelds, as Brian put it, were once again "captive in a situation beyond their control."

That night Brian sent out an email to update everyone. Responses poured in immediately. Brian wrote that the expressions of concern meant a lot to Carol and that she asked him to convey to all who had sent good wishes that she was thrilled to receive them.

Upon his visit the next morning he was pleased to find that an adjustment to Carol's medication was giving her temporary pain relief. They scrolled through the photos he had taken of his trip to Calgary. They talked about the Peacekeepers' Ceremony and their friends who had attended, like Maureen Eykelenboom, Jim Davis, Don Ethell, the force behind the making of Peacekeepers Park, and of course Brian's new acquaintance Padre Monpas. Brian brought cups of crushed ice to soothe Carol's dry throat and he was thoughtful enough to print photographs of Mikey so she could see her beloved dog.

Brian said they shared a few laughs but they also talked openly. "She was tired, and we talked about the future as if there was to be one, and once again her spirits were high, her outlook was positive, although I sensed that she was at the end of her tether with the pain."

Uncertain times like these force couples to talk about issues most pressing. The conversation pivoted around their sons, grandsons, and Mikey. The future of the Izzy Doll project weighed heavily on Carol's heart also, and she wanted to ensure it would be in good hands should something happen to her. There was someone Carol believed would be perfect; a devoted woman she had never met in person but who had become an ally and advocate of the Izzy Dolls. At Carol's request, Brian drove home to make an urgent phone call to Shirley O'Connell, who had been coordinating the Izzy Doll efforts in Southern Ontario. He brought back Shirley's answer, a commitment to the Izzy Dolls and to her friend. Brian said Carol was visibly relieved that Mark's legacy could continue now with Shirley's leadership.

"I kissed her and said that I would see her in the morning."

That night Dave and Lynn Breese, who Brian described as friends who lent their unwavering support, stopped in at the house just after visiting Carol. Carol had told their friends that she could not take much more of the pain and that she was ready to surrender and be with Mark. They said she had spoken calmly and rationally despite her discomfort.

At 8:50 p.m. Wednesday, August 15, 2007, a shocked nurse called from the hospital to inform Brian that Carol had passed. Brian recorded the time of the grave news and sat in front of his computer later that night, as he always had during stressful times, and vented to his friends and imparted the jarring outcome of the day's end.

"Those who know me intimately, and I must confess that there are few who really do, will know that another piece of my heart was suddenly wrenched from me tonight, and over our long relationship and the events that have occurred in our lives, know also that I do not have too many pieces left to spread around. Our constant bantering and seemingly unstructured relationship of 48 years must have seemed to many an anomaly of wonder. But our love for each other was private and real and our very own. I have lost the best thing that ever happened to me, and am still in shock over the suddenness and intensity of the last four days."

Brian wrote the probable cause was peritoneal carcinomatosis, likely due to pancreatic cancer, and said he asked about an autopsy. Carol's doctor suggested the option of donating her corneas to the eye bank as they were in dire need.

"Those who knew Carol know what her immediate answer would have been, and so I signed the papers for the corneal donation in lieu of the autopsy. I know that is what she would have wished for in a heartbeat, and so her vision will live on in more than one or two ways."

Pat flew out from Winnipeg to be with her brother. She had lost a friend in her sister-in-law and she understood best how this would affect her brother.

It seemed the unexplainable was happening daily to Brian. The single red rose that had miraculously appeared in their yard sparked an email to Padre Monpas, Jim Davis, and me.

"I went out to the yard the afternoon after her death, and there was a crimson rose, single and bright, directly in line with Carol's bedroom window, and never before has this particular rose bloomed in our yard. Would you care to explain this to me??"

From a lifetime habit of searching for the logic in everything, Brian was still poised to debate, but as the Padre said in a conversation with me years later, although Brian was not a religious man he had enough honesty that he would recognize the work of the spiritual.

No one can say with certainty that this rose was a message of love from his life's partner and the psychic he had learned to appreciate, but to all of us watching, it sure felt like it.

✳✳✳

Brian's first decision was to keep the family's grief private. When the doctor pointed out that many people would be deprived of showing their respect and love if there was not a public memorial, Brian changed his mind. He began the process of organizing a memorial for Carol and commented how grateful he felt for the hands–on support of 19 Wing Comox Chief Warrant Officer Lloyd Hodgins and his staff. They worked together to arrange a service that represented Carol's lifetime contributions.

I thought about the suddenness of Carol's death, and now with 20/20 hindsight wondered whether Brian regretted his trip to Calgary. The answer came in an email Brian sent to Padre Monpas, and copied me and Jim Davis. I read between the lines. In it, Brian talked about how the Padre had been brought into his life for a reason, which had now become apparent. He wrote that God had made it possible for their paths to cross "at this very moment in my life when I need more than ever to have impressed on me the unwavering strength of God in his many forms ... without clouding my psyche with organized religion and secular unrest.

"You and I both know that our respective spiritual mentor knew in advance the heartache and trials I personally was to so soon be immersed in." Brian ended the email by asking Father Monpas to lead Carol's memorial.

Brian had been deeply affected by the timely meeting of Padre Monpas during the previous weekend in Calgary. Leigh explains, "Something happened to my dad after my mom died and I think it was related to Padre Monpas." Leigh referred to his father as an agnostic. He said his dad functioned in a sceptical and logical mode and believed that no one possessed the evidence to know the unknown and therefore the unknowable. But he said that after Padre Monpas came into his life his dad was rethinking.

It was Brian's idea that Carol's memorial service coincide with a local event called Boomer's Legacy. Many of the same people who knew the Isfelds would be attending this annual event, so it was reasonable to wait a few weeks until September when they would be there already.

Appropriately, the service was held at the Mark R. Isfeld Secondary School. The day was bright and sunny, reflecting Carol's personality and friends said it was as though Carol had conjured it up from the heavens. The gymnasium was packed with respectful admirers of the mother of the Izzy Doll. Her boys sat in the front row beside their father, Aunt Pat, Aunt Judy, Kelly and Dave and Lynn Breese . Father Monpas led the memorial service; it was a fitting tribute to Carol.

THE FINAL GOOD-BYE

"Please forgive me," "I forgive you," "Thank you," and "I love you."

Ira Byock M.D. Author of The Four Things That Matter Most

It is my experience that there exists a law of nature whereby after a loved one dies, life callously proceeds as if nothing at all has happened. It is an uncomfortable force that pushes a person to adjust and thereby survive. For Brian it was difficult to wander the empty house decorated by Carol's hand and see reminders of his wife at every turn. So in October, with Mikey in the passenger seat, the two lonely 'boys' embarked on a road trip. Meandering through the Rockies and across the rolling prairies, their destination was Edmonton to see his sons Leigh and Glenn, and then to Winnipeg where Pat and her family had relocated.

I had asked Brian if he would like to do an online edit for the booklet accompanying the CD I was working on. *In Harm's Way* was a collection of songs about legacy projects of soldiers' families. It was a good project to keep him busy, he certainly knew the content and I had learned to trust his meticulous eye for detail. He had agreed, and we had kept in regular communication. He had been experiencing his own issues with stomach pain for months and he said he would see a doctor when he returned from his travels.

Leigh explained that during his visit, his dad showed his protective side with a surprise gesture. Brian could fathom how the nature of a national project could be potentially stressful so he extended a verbal waiver that would release his boys from the pressure and guilt of carrying on their parents' project. He told Leigh that should the Izzy Doll project impact his and Glenn's lives in a negative way, they had his permission to let it go.

Leigh clarified that although his dad was generous with his statement, he told Brian that the Izzy Doll project was important to them and they would do whatever they could to help it grow.

Brian returned from his travels with an urgency to investigate the cause of the relentless pain that was now plaguing him night and day. He followed through with a medical and tests. Pat emailed me that the diagnosis was colon cancer. Surgery had been scheduled for November 30. The doctors were optimistic.

Dave Breese sat next to Brian in the doctor's waiting room browsing through the small pile of magazines. He had made a promise to his buddy that he would not be alone through this. As it turned out, the prognosis was not optimistic. The cancer had perforated Brian's colon and the doctors had given him two months to live. Dave and Lynn would be beside their friend every step of the way.

Lynn called me with the news. I shook my head at how soon the Isfeld family had been dealt another blow just months after losing Carol. It seemed someone left fairness out when drawing up the laws of nature.

Pat flew out once again to be with Brian. When she called to say her plane had landed, Dave noticed that Brian relaxed knowing she was there. Leigh said his dad could be cantankerous at the best of times and now the incessant pain was causing this proud and independent man to rely heavily on his sister, who became the receptacle for his irritable overflow. Visitors marvelled at her unlimited patience and understanding in the wake of everyone's suffering, including her own.

Brian was adamant that people not send flowers or other such gifts. Many of us accepted the window of opportunity for one last good-bye. I came out from Alberta, Jim Davis flew in from Nova Scotia, and Sophie Richard and Padres Monpas from Ontario. Brian opted to remain at home as long as he could. It was hard to watch him pace the floor, for there was no position that would ease the chronic ache. Pat said he listened to his music constantly, which served as a useful distraction from the pain. He paced while he hummed and occasionally a grin came over his tired face as he sung the racy lyrics from one of his old military songs.

Jim Davis was glad to have the chance to see Brian one last time and he said a visit from Sophie was just what Brian needed. Brian was fond of Sophie and it seemed she could always reach him.

About her visit Sophie said, "Brian has touched our heart in a special way; he left his mark and will be missed by our Program and our bereavement group. Two weeks prior to his death I visited Brian and he gave me his final instructions.... to carry on!"

Much has been published about life end stages; self-reflection, the process of letting go, and the re-evaluating of priorities as the hourglass drains. It had been characteristic of Carol and Mark to demonstrate their affection and express their love readily, but for Brian expressing his feelings had always been a bridge he was hesitant to cross. Now there was willingness and an urgency to say what needed to be said.

Perhaps he was thinking about how Carol could always say the right thing, or perhaps it was the Padre's support that strengthened his resolve. The fact was Brian did cross that bridge to deliver his messages. Leigh said, "My Dad called my brother Glenn and told him he loved him, which was something my Dad never did."

Dave Breese spoke softly as he remembered the final weeks he had spent with his long-time friend. He said Brian had accepted his fate, and he also told of an unlikely show of tenderness while taking his regular dusk 'til dawn shift at the hospital. In the early hours of the morning Brian woke up, and as they often did the two men manoeuvred down the halls and through the doors for the last sensory pleasure Brian could still enjoy, a smoke.

"It was a production getting Brian downstairs and outside," said Dave.

Once Brian was sitting comfortably on the hospital bench he turned to his friend and said in his now frail and hoarse voice, "Give me your hand."

Dave remembers that physical touch was so unlike Brian he was startled. He reached out his hand and Brian intertwined and locked their fingers together. Brian told him how much he appreciated his friendship and all he and Lynn had done for him and Carol. "It was hard not to tear up," said Dave.

Then Brian looked up and with a sly grin and perfect timing executed his classic sarcasm, "If they could see us now, holding hands." Their laughter broke the tension and Brian was safely back in his emotional comfort zone.

***

Leigh arrived at his parents' home and took his turn in the rotation of his father's care. He told of something that had happened on his watch. Brian had awoken and calmly began to describe a comforting dream he had just had. No doubt the potent medication added some Technicolor but the imagery was his very own; the characters were his loved ones riding in a multi-coloured train flying through the sky like Santa's reindeer. At the windows of each car were familiar faces. Carol and Mark were there, smiling. His Mom, Steinunn, and his Father, Arilius, were there too and others who had gone before him. He looked into Leigh's face and with conviction in his voice said, "I'm going somewhere good."

Soon after that, the pain became too severe for Brian's body and mind to endure. He slipped into a comatose state and nature took its course. Brian left this world and joined his loved ones on the heavenly train waiting in the sky for his last road trip home.

***

Brian said that kindred spirits meet eventually. In an email to me he wrote: "Have no doubt that Mark, Boomer and Paul are now friends. And now the crowning glory from yours truly… notes about the "band of Brothers" Boomer, Mark, Paul and all the others." And he included this poem he had written about the three young soldiers, but now, after his death, it also speaks of him.

Weep not for us when we are gone,
Remember us and we'll live on.
Our earthly tasks, though they are done,
Must be continued by other ones.
Weep for them

For they must face,
The pitfalls of our human race.
Weep for widows, and moms and dads,
Siblings and friends that we all had.
Weep for them

For in the abyss of their very hearts,
There lies a growing void;
Of shattered dreams, now unfulfilled
And hopes for us that never will
Be seen by those we loved.
Weep for them

Voids that can't be filled with clichés
Long and short;
Time does not heal, it numbs the brain,
And in so doing it dulls the pain
Of those we left behind
Weep for them

We soldiers are together now,
We're new made friends in this hereafter,
We joke and play and know much laughter
and wish for those we left behind
to know we've saved a place beside us

And until then please carry on;
Remember us as we once were,

As little boys with hair so fair
And pockets full of who knows what
And how, and when, and where.

Weep not for us for we live on
In hearts and minds and song.
We'll be together soon enough
And we'll play catch up with all the stuff
That we had to leave behind.

Brian Isfeld

(And that's enough for now. Comments are elicited,
and don't cry when you read it.) Brian

CHAPTER 4

BOOMER'S LEGACY

CORPORAL ANDREW 'BOOMER' EYKELENBOOM

There is one thing that I could not live without and that is Hope. A hope for the future, a hope in that somehow this crazy journey we are on is for a purpose far unknown to us.

Maureen Eykelenboom, 2010

Carol and Brian lived in Courtney, Maureen and Hans Eykelenboom in Comox, twin cities located on Vancouver Island. The couples were strangers to each other until a fateful happening that caused their paths to cross.

Brian emailed me the following details of the tragic death of a soldier he referred to as one of their neighbours.

"Cpl. Andrew Eykelenboom, 23, was an army medic who was killed in a suicide attack in Afghanistan on Aug. 11, 2006. Known by colleagues as "Boomer", Eykelenboom was serving with the First Field Ambulance unit based out of CFB Edmonton. It was his last mission at the end of a 7 month tour."

Action oriented, and with a desire to help others, Andrew had trained as a firefighter while he was still in high school. His friends commented that Boomer studied hard, played hard, and could disarm anyone with his mirthful grin. After graduating from Grade 12 he made a decision to join the army. It was only months after 9-11 and the notion of her youngest son in a war zone, prompted questions from his mother about his timing. Andrew's rebuttal was, "Well, Mom, if that's the case I'm going to be needed more than ever."

"That was who he was," explained Maureen. She continued with another memory. While driving through Edmonton on a biting winter's afternoon, Andrew, in the passenger seat, sat with his shoulders hunched over, shivering, and rubbing his two hands together for warmth. "Where are your gloves and toque I gave you for Christmas?" she asked.

Andrew hesitated, then confessed, "I gave them to a homeless man. He needed them more than I did."

There were many occasions when Andrew eagerly lost himself in the moment helping others, particularly children and the disabled. In a letter he sent home while serving in Afghanistan he wrote, "Putting a smile on a child's face is the most rewarding thing about this tour." Andrew had a strong sense of duty in responding to the needs in the world, and he died doing just that.

The loss of their son and brother had forever changed the Eykelenboom family as they knew it. Friends, and even strangers, reached out to them during their darkest days as they tried to adjust to their new reality without Boomer. Tim Goddard, the father of Captain Nichola Goddard who was killed in combat in Afghanistan just months prior to Andrew's death, had telephoned to extend his empathy and support. Although they had never met, the Goddards shared a set of circumstances with the Eykelenbooms few other parents could identify with.

***

The news of Boomer's death sent shock waves throughout his circle of family and friends. People immediately wanted to do something that would honour this young soldier. Two of his mother's friends Pamela Jolin and Val Wall, knew that lives of infants and small children could be saved with knitted caps that preserved body heat when night temperatures dropped. They began knitting soft, warm head coverings they nicknamed Boomer Caps. Just as the Izzy Doll charmed its crafters, the story of the Boomer Caps stirred knitting needles to action for the Boomer Cap cause. Individuals and knitting groups from churches, women's organizations, and service clubs such as Soroptimist International (of which Maureen is a member), responded.

Since the Boomer Cap Project began in 2006, more than 138,000 Boomer Caps have been created. They are distributed, along with Izzy Dolls, by military personnel as well as by humanitarian groups like ICROSS Canada. Boomer Caps have travelled to Afghanistan, Guatemala, Romania, Uganda and other parts of Africa and the Canadian knitters say it is satisfying to send something that will bring joy to the children.

***

Brian Isfeld and Vancouver North MP John Duncan were instrumental in changing how the Memorial Cross was delivered, so now, more than a decade later, Maureen could choose how she wanted to receive hers. She decided on an informal gathering in her home.

A dozen pair of shiny black military boots lined up inside their front entrance, reminding Maureen of twenty-four polished soldiers at attention. She also remembered a barrage of mixed emotion about this ceremony. The bereaved mother described the sickening feeling she felt, accepting a medal "for the death of my son." And when people thanked her for her sacrifice, she said she wanted to cry out, "Andrew made the sacrifice. I didn't."

She busied herself with hostess duties, trying to deflect the intense emotions she was feeling. She couldn't allow herself to slow down lest she erupt in tears or anger, or both. Additional drinks were needed for the houseful of guests so she slipped downstairs to get more. On her way back up, a capricious impulse dared her to stop at the twenty-four leather boots, laces perfect and peering straight ahead. An overwhelming whim to mix up the sizes came over her. It was something her playful son Andrew would have done. She smiled. She knew he was with her.

***

The program of H.O.P.E. touched Maureen's life through Jim Davis, who had initiated regular conversations with her. She said what others had echoed; that she was comforted knowing that she was not alone. This knowledge enabled her to move forward — something she thought she would never be able to do.

Their relationship had come about because of their losses, but Jim Davis considered their friendship as another gift from his son; a gift that continued to manifest in so many ways. He recalled how it was surreal to hear Maureen relate stories about Andrew. There were so many similarities between their sons. Jim called it uncanny; it was an unexpected comfort for him.

There were similarities between these parents also. After the loss of their sons, both Jim and Maureen had thought about beginning a legacy project. Maureen knew it had to be something that Boomer would have been proud of and that would best complement the role of a soldier. She started Boomer's Legacy Fund and collaborated with Jim in determining what it would look like. They decided on a resource fund whereby soldiers could requisition resources and items that could help the local civilians survive and rebuild their lives. Rather than turn a blind eye to suffering, which would feed a sense of powerlessness, a soldier could be a catalyst for positive change by improving living conditions for victims of war. This, in turn, helped to make the soldier feel empowered.

Money raised through Boomer's Legacy Fund is allocated to the Assistance to Afghanistan Trust Fund (AATF). The AATF was established in the fall of 2006 under General Rick Hillier's command and is managed by the Canadian Forces Joint Task Force through the Provincial Reconstruction Team. In 2011 Maureen announced that "the Assistance to Afghanistan Trust Fund has been renamed Boomer's Trust." Funds are available to our military members whereever they are deployed anywhere in the world.

Jim Davis explained that Boomer's Legacy was also an opportunity for soldiers to "promote Canadian goodwill in foreign climates of indifference." A politically neutral organization, Boomer's Legacy Fund provides aid to civilians regardless of ethnic or religious background.

Early projects supported by Boomer's Legacy were shoes for kids, a generator for a water pump, a herd of sheep and even medical operations — all prompted directly by soldiers' requests. To date the Fund has expanded to include special projects such as a store in Kandahar selling locally made merchandise, the first of its kind to be operated by Afghan women.

Brian and Carol Isfeld were proud of Maureen's endeavours with Boomer's Legacy. They could attest to the fact that war had impacted their son. Mark had struggled with feelings of despair and anger after witnessing the starving children, victims crippled after a landmine incident, and the elderly abandoned with no means of support. This new fund would go a long way to offset the sense of helplessness, seen as a symptom of PTSD and OSI.

Boomer's Legacy Fund has certainly absorbed much of Maureen's energy. She and her troop of volunteers have organized annual gala events and bike tours to raise awareness and donations.

In 2010, celebrity W. Brett Wilson from the CBC television series *Dragon's Den* hosted a garden party in Calgary. Canadians showed their generosity by contributing a whopping $265,000 to Boomer's Legacy Fund.

This Canadian project benefits both the receiver and the giver. I have come to believe that this grassroots initiative, born from the pain of greiving families to make sense of their loss and based on the belief that we can build a better world, could very well become one of the most powerful tools for peace and healing on this planet.

Since Andrew's death, a lot has transpired to give Maureen a broader understanding of her son's decision to enlist. She accepted an opportunity to travel to Afghanistan, where she shook hands with soldiers working in the field and heard their stories. The bigger picture emerged, and she commented about her new insights:

Gordon and Maureen Eykelenboom with W. Brett Wilson

"They see they may have an opportunity to make a greater difference in the world, to go wherever the country sends them — to keep our country strong by making the world a better place."

Maureen said she came to understand what Andrew and many other Canadians throughout history truly believed — that their actions could make a difference. "I have such an appreciation of what our ancestors did. I never got it before. There is nothing more fundamentally important than your footprint on the earth. If your action can afford to give the generation to follow a better life, not a bigger TV, but a free life, it's worth it."

The death of a soldier is different than a civilian death. Bereaved parents and families suffer through their grief in the public eye. Maureen points out that when a soldier is killed, a phone call from the prime minister and the media attention makes it more public. Civilian opinions and judgments on the politics of soldiers' postings, public outcry to bring troops home after a soldier's death, and even the opposite reaction — the apathy, and people who don't want to know anything — all add to the barrage of pressure on these families.

Marriage can be affected as well, either by bringing partners closer together or driving them apart. Siblings can feel isolated, withdrawing into their own world, while others might act out or speak out trying to communicate their feelings.

While on a trip to Calgary in 2010 to visit her son Gordon and his family, Maureen scheduled a meeting with me. Nicely dovetailing our coffee time between shopping with her daughter-in-law and grandchildren, we had time to sit and talk. Maureen looked more relaxed than the last time I saw her. I commented on this and asked her how she was handling everything. Between husband, children, grandchildren and the whirlwind of administrative duties involved in running the Boomer's Legacy Fund, and coordinating Boomer Caps, I could understand how chaotic her life must be.

"Hans wanted to make the world go away," explained Maureen about her husband's path through grief. Her response was the opposite of his and her extroverted personality craved projects and activity. The steady stream of dedicated volunteers and media coverage brought the world closer.

Elbows propped up on the table, her hands held her coffee cup close to her lips. She set the mug down, pondering her next statement, then looked me straight in the eye. "The worst thing someone said to me was 'at least you have two other sons.'" Maureen said she felt indignant over that remark until one day her own son expressed something similar. With an air of peace about her, she told me the story of how her eyes had been opened wide.

Focusing her energy on the legacy projects, and having a constant need to talk about her deceased son, had caused her other sons Steven and Gordon to wonder if their mother had forgotten about them. Trying to hold on to as many memories as was humanly possible she was prospecting for more stories about Andrew when Gordon turned to her and in a serious tone announced, "You have two other sons. Andrew wasn't perfect you know."

Gordon's comment caught his mother off guard and she internalized his words. It took courage for Gordon to speak out, and it was his statement that moved his mom toward an epiphany. "I never thought I was portraying Andrew as perfect ... I realized my world was revolving around Andrew and I was missing out." Motivated to create some goodness out of a tragedy, she had been moving in a singular direction, unaware of how alienated her family had felt.

Maureen said that it took time and a conscious effort to restore the family equilibrium that had been paved over with her good intentions. She said she realized that, "I am still called Mom" and that her role as a grandmother is precious. It takes a conscious awareness to be fully present, Maureen explains, and she credits her faith as the key to her efforts.

"I found my way back in prayer and in the comfort of my strong faith knowing Andrew is in a better place. I learned to love Hans like I was supposed to and not be so bent on helping make a change because of what I lost. Now I can let it go and be with the grandchildren."

She still remains a loyal steward of the Boomer's Legacy projects and is now active in the program of H.O.P.E. supporting other families with a mother's empathy and with the message that they are not alone.

As Maureen hugs her grandson, born a year after Andrew's death, and takes his littler brother's hand, her love radiates. Wisdom has blossomed from the black soil of pain, and in her maturity she has grown to accept the full circle of the puzzling process we call life. And death.

CHAPTER 5

THE STORY OF ICROSS CANADA

Millions of Aids orphans in Africa today
Need your support and need you to pray
Kids need painkillers, ointments and more
And medical dressings to cover each sore
Children hug wee dolls to help ease their pain
Immune systems fail, and good health drains
open ulcer sores upon the skin soon appears
Mom and Dad have gone. All alone with fears
The 'izzy African Comfort Doll it is dearly loved
Through suffering tears the wee doll is hugged
Upon their little faces are the wee smiles of joy
Bringing comfort to orphaned wee girls and boys

Billy Willbond, Saanichton B.C.

Billy and Lynne Willbond

RETIRING —INTO WORKS OF MERCY

"My Gr. 3 teacher Miss Minnie Loftis would say, "Sit up straight you big, bold, brassy, boob." She is the one who saw me singing and writing skipping songs for the girls and she directed me by saying, "You can write poetry for yourself and others OR you can write to make a difference." I've written thousands of poems since then, mostly to make a difference."

Billy Willbond

Some called the tattered young WWII vets sleeping under the bridge in Northwest Ottawa "shell-shocked." By day they would deliver flyers for a pittance. It was just enough for the cheap wine that helped them escape the flashbacks of the bloody conflicts that still haunted them.

It was the late 1940s and no one understood post-traumatic stress disorder, only that most soldiers came back from the war changed and many had difficulty getting their lives back. Living nearby, Mrs. Veroncia (Monica) Willbond would make enough Irish stew for her own brood of nine children and her Scottish husband as well as extra to feed these men. She carried no expectations or judgment of their circumstance.

Billy grew up watching his Irish mom perform acts of what she called "works of mercy." Many years later, several of these once homeless former soldiers, with their lives rebuilt, stood at the back of the church at Mrs. Willbond's funeral, thankful for her free meals and her kindness.

Today her Bible sits on the bookcase at Billy's house, and he points out a verse circled by his mother: *The needy will not be forgotten, nor the hope of the afflicted perish.* Psalms 9:19

This became the motto Billy chose for the relief organization he formed after a series of climactic events unexpectedly redirected his life.

***

Billy served as a Peacekeeper until retiring from the Canadian Forces then he worked another twenty-three years at a desk job at a 'cop shop.' During his careers as both a military and civilian Peacekeeper, Billy had seen the worst of human behaviours and what people were capable of doing to each other. Billy had a profile and demeanour akin to Santa Claus, but he admits he had distrust and little patience for the bleeding hearts of the world who wore masks of deception.

Like his mother, Billy believed in acts of kindness, and he and his wife, Lynne, also valued the sacrifices made by our soldiers and their families. On August 9, 1995, National Peacekeepers Day, Billy and Lynne's family hosted a tea at the James Bay Tea Room in Victoria. An invitation was extended to Brian and Carol

Mary, Sandra, Bridey, and Paula

Isfeld, who also lived on Vancouver Island. It was here the Willbonds met the Isfelds for the first time, enjoying a unique fellowship and respect, and sharing stories, poems, and friendship over tea. The Isfelds formed a bond with Billy and Lynne's daughters that would later see the Izzy Doll enter Billy's life in a big way. But not quite yet.

Billy, the father, the grandfather, and the poet, was anticipating retirement and all the free time he would have to take hunting trips, spend with his grandchildren, and write poetry. But with a mortgage to worry about, retirement was still in the distant future.

***

In August 1998, Billy and Lynne saved up to make a journey to visit Billy's brother, who was working in East Africa for the Canadian International Development Agency (CIDA). The trip was dual purpose. They would also lay wreaths donated by the Royal Canadian Legion on the Canadian soldiers' graves in the Commonwealth Graveyard outside Nairobi, Kenya. A local Jesuit priest, Brother Michael Meegan, had agreed to officiate at the service and said a prayer at the gravesite. Billy and Lynne, as the surrogate family, stood proudly in front of the crosses of the Canadian soldiers who would never be returning home.

After the service, Brother Michael extended an invitation for the Willbonds to come back to his home for tea. Referring to the life-changing chain of events that would follow, Billy, with a big grin on his face and tongue in cheek reflected, "That's when I made the first mistake."

Brother Michael escorted his new friends into his world filled with anguish, poverty and pain. Orphaned infants and toddlers were everywhere, crowded in cribs with end-stage HIV AIDS ulcers, whimpering in pain. Billy remembers how heart wrenching it felt to hear the cries and sobs of the babies.

He blurted out, "Brother Michael, what can we do?"

Brother Michael responded, "Billy, when you have nothing, anything is wonderful."

Billy repeated his plea, "No, Brother Michael, what can we do?"

Brother Michael replied that a half of an aspirin can help give a baby a good night's sleep, and that they always needed ointment and bandages.

Lynne had seen pain and suffering in her job as a nurse, but the sight and sounds of these frail orphans was both shocking and numbing. The lack of healing medicines, painkillers, and inadequate facilities was disturbing. There had to be something they could do.

ON A MISSION

"Overcoming poverty is not a gesture of charity. It is an act of justice. It is the protection of a fundamental human right, the right to dignity and a decent life . . ."

Nelson Mandela

Billy and Lynne flew back home, on a mission. Billy began hunting and tracking in ways he hadn't anticipated before their trip to Africa. The Willbonds went hunting for the best prices they could find for bandages and ointment and tracked down every sale for aspirins. And they used funds from their own bank accounts to make the purchases. Stacks upon stacks of boxes were readied for sending, but because the costs of shipping were so prohibitive, Billy used his resources and contacted a higher power. "After I got back from Africa I wrote to PM Jean Chretien asking how I could get medical supplies to Africa — he passed my request to the MND, who passed it to the CDS who passed it to the head of the Airforce who authorized shipment through the Admiral at Canadian Forces Base Esquimalt. It went from here to Trenton and was placed on Hercs heading for Africa — thanks to the PM of this great country — unfortunately there is no money for that sort of thing now."

The Willbonds remained realistic, very aware that their efforts were just a drop in the ocean of need, but it was their drop in the ocean and they were compelled to try. Billy said, "Lynn went to Costco and Walmart and bought huge boxes of loss leader sale items." They earmarked the supplies for CIDA and prepared more packages. Billy did use his guns again, but not as he had once planned. Choosing from his collection, he sold them off one by one to pay the high cost of shipping the parcels overseas.

In total they had sent an astounding 400 boxes of medical supplies. Other people may have patted themselves on the back and retreated into their comfortable Canadian lifestyle after making such generous donations. But not Billy and Lynne. They had no desire to back off. There was too much to do. Seeing the faces of the helpless orphans had altered their lives forever.

While in Kenya, Brother Michael had told them about the work of ICROSS International, a volunteer-based organization he had co founded. An acronym for the International Community of Relief of Starvation and Suffering, it seemed to say exactly what the Willbonds felt drawn to do; relieve starvation and suffering.

***

Like the Isfelds, the Willbonds' story is about the human spirit rising above the shock and despair of the suffering in our world. It is also about how a higher power can intervene to validate our direction when our intention is clear and our spirit convinced. Billy and Lynne were convinced that they needed to be part of a concerted effort, combining their drop in the ocean with the drops of others. They weren't sure how it was going to happen, but they were committed to creating a wave of hope to ease at least some of the suffering in the world.

As many Canadians do, Billy and Lynne bought a 649 lottery ticket. It could have been chance or destiny. Or it could have been providence that saw their winning number take home $120,000 — coincidentally just enough to pay off their mortgage of $119,000. They were shocked and happy. Billy paid off the mortgage, retired from the 'cop shop,' and committed his retirement years to helping, as he puts it in his Celtic way, "The poorest of the poor on this battered and wee bleeding planet."

Billy took the first steps to organizing an ICROSS Canada chapter, trusting that there would be others who would join their humanitarian efforts. It would operate independently of other ICROSS chapters around the world.

To begin spreading the word, Billy wrote an article about their trip to Africa for the membership newsletter of the Canadian Association of Veterans in United Nations Peacekeeping (CAVUNP). The story of Brother Michael and the Masai stirred an interest with his Peacekeeper brothers. As a result many joined Billy's efforts with ICROSS Canada. The pledge of ICROSS Canada reads:

We will ease the suffering and feed the victims of poverty on this battered and bleeding planet. We will accomplish this by gathering material and financial resources to meet the needs of the poorest of the poor.

The plan of ICROSS Canada was to seek out surplus from Canadian hospitals and clinics that were renovating or rebuilding. These donations were excellent upgrades and additions for Third World clinics. The ICROSS Canada volunteers worked their plan by gathering, organizing, and loading trucks with surplus wheelchairs, crutches, walkers, and medical and diagnostic equipment. On one occasion Billy was able to secure a used operating theatre. Cash donations would go towards medicines, painkillers, bandages, and salve, or anything else that might be requested.

Lynne remained nursing and volunteered her spare time to ICROSS Canada contributing as required, particularly in managing the accounting.

Corruption in third world governments and aid organizations regularly highlighted in the media was of great concern to Billy. Above all, he was committed to making sure that ICROSS Canada was accountable to Canadians and that their donations reached the intended recipients. To avoid top-heavy administration costs that would drain their funds, one rule was established that said it all: "No one at ICROSS CANADA gets paid; therefore, all donated monies go towards the shipping of life-saving and ease-suffering medical supplies to the global village on our battered and bleeding wee planet."

Next, Billy decided to bring in the big guns. He picked up the phone and called a former commander he had served under in Cypress, thirty years earlier. Now a Major General, Lewis (Lew) MacKenzie was surprised to hear from a former soldier. The formation of ICROSS Canada and the scope of its humanitarian outreach interested him so much that he accepted the position as patron of the Canadian chapter. Lew assisted in obtaining the Canadian charity number for income tax purposes and donor receipts, and the Major General's high profile and reputation was an important asset to this growing charity.

THE HIGH COST OF DELIVERY

"The growth of the warehouse has been a small miracle."

Leif Wergeland, Saanich counsellor and CRW co-founder

The high cost of delivery was a constant issue with Billy. A percentage of incoming charitable donations that could have been used to buy medical supplies had to cover the cost of shipping. Billy was in a state of alert for the least expensive and most secure method of shipment, so when a referral came in, he acted immediately.

Dell Marie Wergeland was the director of the Compassionate Resource Warehouse operating out of Victoria, B.C. Coincidently, this volunteer-based group had its roots anchored in a heartfelt experience, also.

Dell, her husband, and brother-in-law were part of a volunteer group who traveled to Honduras to provide relief aid in the aftermath of Hurricane Mitch in 1998. They were confronted by the devastation but felt inadequate, because of the lack of resources, to meet the needs of the victims. Dell was a nurse so she worked in the aid station. When the supplies the volunteers had brought ran out, she was struck with the abundance in Canada and the useful "stuff" we throw out every day — "stuff" that could be used here and now.

After returning home to Vancouver Island, a decision was made to send a large shipping container with humanitarian supplies to Honduras. It took eighteen months to gather the items to help the struggling victims of Hurricane Mitch. The group was elated, and as a result the Compassionate Resource Warehouse was formed. Initially sponsored by the Church of the Nazerene, now CRW is a stand-alone charitable organization. It has grown into its own community of volunteers, mostly retired seniors. These hardworking volunteers, many of whom were raised during the Great Depression, knew what it was like to be hungry and to have very little.

Experienced fixers and recyclers, they have a knack for making second-hand donations look almost new. They stack and pack a 5,000 square foot warehouse with supplies such as clothes, school desks, books, medical supplies, blankets, and linens. They then transfer the items into large shipping containers bound for locations in Central and South America, Mexico, Africa, Pakistan, Tibet, and the Philippines.

CRW has partnered with trustworthy organizations to ship more than 310 containers at a cost of between $5,000 and $10,000 per container. ICROSS Canada has allied with CRW; their partnership has been an answer to Billy and Lynne's prayers.

ICROSS CANADA MEETS THE IZZY DOLL

"The Izzy Dolls cannot be bought or sold."
The Izzy Doll Rule

Meanwhile, back on the home front, life's twists and turns refocused Billy and Lynne's attention. Shae-lyn, one of their grandchildren, was diagnosed with a heart condition and needed surgery. Even knowing they had the best medical care could not allay their worries and stress. It was the circumstances beyond their control that prompted a prayer request, a familiar strategy they called on to help confront the unknown.

Carol Isfeld was on their email list of friends. Not only did she commit to pray for Shae-lyn, she also made a gift that had a track record to comfort and bring a smile to a child's face. Carol delivered a little girl Izzy Doll to five-year-old Shae-lyn's bedside.

Sandra, Shae-lyn's aunt, was delighted with her niece's reaction to her new toy and in the craftsmanship of the crocheted gift. Sandra and Carol talked about the pattern. Sandra talked with Billy and one thing led to another. It was decided that Izzy Dolls would be included in their shipments to the orphaned and the poor. Carol said she thought Mark would be very proud indeed.

Depending on its destination, an Izzy Doll took on a different name; In Africa, it was called The Izzy African Comfort Doll, in other locations it was The Izzy Comfort Doll. To stop anyone from trying to commercialize the Izzy Doll, Billy and Carol decided to make it a rule that Izzy Dolls could not be bought or sold.

Billy sent emails looking for knitters to make dolls for the neediest children on the planet. The response was steady. Carol urged the crafters to try other designs and to choose darker coloured yarns for different skin colors so the children could better identify with the doll. The Izzy Comfort dolls were all shapes and sizes, bright and colourful, soft and cuddly.

As well as a humanitarian gift, The Izzy Doll was also practical and cost effective. Not only could the dolls be created from leftover pieces of yarn, they were also inexpensive to ship. Because they were small and soft they could be used to package fragile medicines and breakable lab equipment, such as test tubes and glass vials in Physicians' Travel Packs (PTPs). Previous packaging material like bubble pads and Styrofoam 'peanuts' were useless waste upon arrival, but the Izzy Doll 'packaging' was welcomed, recycled, wanted, and loved.

***

1998 had been an unbelievable year for the Willbonds. Within a few months after returning from their August trip to the Congo, Billy and Lynne had purchased and sent several shipments of aid and won a lottery ticket that allowed Billy to 'retire' into works of mercy. By October 1 they had initiated the

Canadian chapter of 1CROSS and, then, established the Izzy Doll as their humanitarian organization's mascot.

Since they had made a decision to help ease the suffering in the world, it was as though miracles were helping them along their way. And they felt grateful for another blessing; Shae-lyn made a full recovery. Her Izzy Doll sits in a place of honour in her bedroom.

THE HIGH COST OF CORRUPTION

"Corruption is both a major cause and a result of poverty around the world."

Anup Shah, www.globalissues.com

It was widely acknowledged that corruption hampers humanitarian aid and foreign investment in developing countries. ICROSS Canada can testify to this corruption and its high cost. As shipments entered the country of destination, there were sometimes surprise taxes, kickbacks for corrupt officials, or payoffs before the goods would be allowed to pass.

CTV Television's popular investigative series called *W5* filmed a documentary about ICROSS Canada in 2005. Called *Heart of Darkness*, the story followed Billy and a jam-packed container from where it had been loaded, at the Compassionate Resource Warehouse, to its destination in Kenya. When the container arrived in Kenya, a government bureaucrat would not allow it to pass; a bogus import duty of $6,000 U.S. was demanded. It seemed ironic that aid could travel half way around the world and then be stalled by greedy citizens of the country the aid was sent to help.

In some countries, practices of payouts and scams seem to be cultural and are as accepted as bartering. Therefore, trying to organize humanitarian shipments in countries without laws and regulations is a daunting challenge.

But ICROSS Canada perseveres, and the evidence can be found on the walls and beds of Third World facilities. Stainless steel pots and bowls with St. Josephs Hospital, British Columbia, etched on them sit on shelves behind the operating room in Kajiado at the Maasai Hospital. Vancouver Island Health Authority is tattooed on bed linens that make up the beds in several Congo hospitals. And, attached to many Izzy Comfort Dolls, are tags with the ICROSS Canada logo, a reminder to the recipient of a country that cares.

Author's note: The man known as Brother Michael Meegan, one of the co-founders of ICROSS International, had been the beneficiary of awards and large charitable grants for his work with the people of the Masai. In 2010 he was accused of misappropriation of funds, misrepresenting himself as a qualified physician and a Jesuit, and sexual assault. At the time of publication, these allegations are all under investigation.

When Billy heard this report about the man who had inspired him and Lynne, he was sad and disappointed. However, he remains steadfast in his resolve to maintain a Canadian ICROSS that is accountable and transparent. Billy said that although ICROSS Canada donated supplies to Michael Meegan's clinic, no money was ever sent.

FEED THE HUNGRY PROGRAM

"Give a woman a fish; you have fed her for today. Teach a woman to fish; and you have fed her and her family for a lifetime"

Adaptation of traditional proverb

ICROSS Canada began a project that would teach women how to feed themselves and their families. Feed the Hungry is a program that addresses the root of poverty in what some call the largest slum in the world — Kibera, in Nairobi, Kenya. Women who had been reduced to prostitution to bring in an income were relocated with their children to a fifty-acre parcel of land called the Shamba. Through donations, ICROSS Canada built a school, a well, and set up a solar pump. They supply livestock — goats, rabbits, and chickens — and vegetable seeds so the families can produce their own food. Their new home was developed under the leadership of Canadian Dr. Bridgit Stirling, who is also ICROSS Canada's medical advisor.

Currently she runs a three-year RN training program at the University of Libya. In Billy's words, this program is "to help train, educate and give some independence and job security to young Moslem women who are studying to become RNs and who will make an impact on public health and disease control amongst the poor of their nation."

Carol and Brian knew Bridgit when she was just a little girl. She and her sisters would meet the parents of our fallen Peacekeepers on Peacekeepers' Day at the James Bay Tea House. Bridgit is the youngest daughter of Lynn and Billy Willbond. She continues the "works of mercy" just as her grandmother Monica Willbond did a half a century ago. Granny Willbond would be so proud if she could see her family now.

I.C.R.O.S.S. CANADA'S ANGELS

"The smiles on the children's faces, who receive these dolls, are equalled only by the twinkle in the eyes of our canadian knitters!"

Mike Comeau, Ontario Director, ICROSS Canada

It was Carol Isfeld's view that the benevolent knitters and crafters were all angels rushing in to meet a need. Billy also witnessed the arrival of volunteers who seemed to come from out of the blue. Here are only a few examples of the thousands of Canadian angels working for the relief of starvation and suffering in the world:

"Trapper Cane attended at my residence with a group of CAV members. He gave me the monies for the eye lenses. A neighbour later in the day said, 'Did you have a group of Hell's Angels at your house today?' "No, it was a group of CAV members and actually they are Heaven's Angels. They help Aids orphans and Blind children' was my response."

Billy Willbond

Paul "Trapper" Cane is a modern-day action hero, and his story is another book that needs to be written. He knows what it's like to accept help, he knows all about helping others, and he knows courage.

Trapper's twenty-three-year career with the Princess Patricia's Canadian Light Infantry (PPCLI) ended abruptly after a mid-air parachute accident that almost ended his life. His parachute became entangled with another soldier's chute. Rather than risk his 'brother's' life, he cut himself free knowing he would free fall to his death. Trapper pulled his reserve chute but it wasn't soon enough to break the fall. He smashed into the ground breaking most of his bones — including his spine — and shattering his teeth.

It was a miracle he survived, but doctors told him he would never have the use of his legs again. Riding his motorcycle was therapy for Trapper; his bike was his legs.

Eighteen operations, physical therapy, and several years later, Trapper did walk again. In 2003 he organized a motorcycle unit made up of veterans like himself who had been injured or felt displaced. It also welcomed civilians and women. They formed the Canadian Army Veteran (CAV) Motorcycle Unit and established a motto, *Strength and Honour,* as well as the mission statement, *Ride, have fun, help others.* Since the group's inception the members have raised millions of dollars for various charities including ICROSS Canada and the Tony Stacey Centre for veterans Care.

Billy said of this group, "The CAV helped us to purchase a CD4 machine which measures HIV and AIDS in a patient's blood, and they helped us purchase a sterilizer and the surgical equipment to perform C sections in our Canadian Medical Clinic Maternity Ward in Engodzi up on Lake Malaw. One woman and one child per week are being saved. Thousands die of complications each year. We are saving a few."

Like Carol Isfeld, Billy is always quick to thank the angels of mercy who work hard for ICROSS Canada. Here is one of his thank you letters, directed at Trapper and the members of the CAV.

Billy with George Dobson (front) one of the many volunteer angels dedicated to ICROSS Canada

"Words cannot express the feelings I have for your wonderful Motor Cycle club's efforts which come from the heart and are raised by the roar of MCs on rides for Charity. You have helped to make a difference with the children of war and the HIV and AIDS orphans and the children of the poor in Africa. You helped us to send meds to the Sudan along with thousands of Izzy African Comfort Dolls and Boomer Caps to places like the Congo, Nigeria, Tanzania, Malawi, Uganda, Cuba, Haiti and the global villages of our battered and bleeding wee planet. Thank You … See you on the open road with the wind at your back and the feeling of freedom that comes with "the ride." Bless you for caring and thank you for sharing."

"General MacKenzie is one of Canada's finest, hardest working and most active humanitarians. He has a schedule that would kill a 20 year old …"

Billy Willbond

Major General Lewis (Lew) MacKenzie: As well as being the patron of ICROSS Canada, Lew has been a tremendous 'soldier' for the organization's projects. He works tirelessly to raise funds including what was needed for the building of a school as well as a shower stall for the families of the Shamba. (Feed The Hungry Project). He also rides and works alongside Trapper and the CAV Motor Cycle Unit to fundraise for CAV charities. He is a man who leads and who others want to follow.

Lewis Mackenzie and Don Ethell

"Few will have the greatness to bend history itself, but each of us can work to change a small portion of events. It is from numberless diverse acts of courage and belief that human history is shaped. "

Robert F. Kennedy

Don Ethell: I wonder if any of the Calgary knitters recognized the man at their front door who had arrived to pick up their homemade Izzy Dolls. I suspect they didn't realize this retirement aged man was not only ICROSS Canada's Alberta director, but also Canada's most experienced and most decorated Peacekeeper. A veteran of fourteen UN Peacekeeping tours, Don Ethell is well known as a humanitarian as well as a proficient soldier.

Don sent me my first Izzy Doll after he had heard the Izzy Doll song. I had not yet met the Isfelds in person, so this doll was my first. I was as thrilled as a kid — thrilled to hold it and to tell its story.

Don was continually "doing for others" by loading trucks with medical surplus earmarked for ICROSS Canada, or as the Chair of Operation Stress Injury Social Structure (OSSIS) or even on a committee to preserve veterans' rights.

As Alberta Director of ICROSS Canada, Don had organized hundreds and hundreds of doll shipments for ICROSS Canada. He even organized a knitters group within his church.

In 2010 Don was made Lieutenant Governor of Alberta and currently serves as Her Majesty the Queen's representative. The Izzy Doll project continues to be very near and dear to his heart; in fact, he keeps an Izzy Doll on his desk in his office in the Legislature.

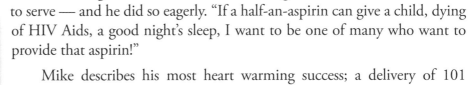

"I took up the Izzy Doll program because I believe in its value and worth. I'm often called 'the Doll Man' but it's not because I'm good looking or sexy (chuckle)."

Mike Comeau

When **Mike Comeau** saw CTV's *Heart of Darkness* he joined ICROSS Canada and immediately began collecting medical equipment for the needy. A man with a sense of humour and heart of gold, he has a deep empathy for others. When his first wife died of cancer at twenty-one years of age he was left to grieve and raise his two baby daughters alone. People had helped him, and he was grateful for their support.

Mike spent twenty-one years in the military and had seen what soldiers see; the destitute children and the victims of conflicts. ICROSS Canada had given Mike, now retired and a grandfather of seven, an outlet

to serve — and he did so eagerly. "If a half-an-aspirin can give a child, dying of HIV Aids, a good night's sleep, I want to be one of many who want to provide that aspirin!"

Mike describes his most heart warming success; a delivery of 101 hospital beds and mattresses to a long-term facility in Cuba. He said he slept well that night knowing there were elderly who no longer had to sleep on cardboard or rusty old beds.

Mike Comeau's name is also synonymous with the ICROSS Canada Izzy Doll project in Ontario. Knitting groups recognize his red GMC truck when it pulls up to the curb. It's white truck-cap sporting the red letter 'ICROSS Canada' signage he purchased himself.

He loads bags of dolls created by more than a thousand knitters from the twenty-one groups in his home province. As well as pickups and sorting he makes presentations, telling the story of the Izzy Doll. Mike liaises with Shirley O'Connell, the new Izzy Doll Mamma, as they coordinate both Izzy Dolls and boomer caps. In 2005 ICROSS Canada presented Mike

Mike with Maria Rydzkowski and Laddie Balon,

with the Humanitarian Award for his commitment. Mike acknowledges that he couldn't do it without his 'tolerent wife, Carol' of thirty years, who supports him in his endeavours.

He says his greatest passion is his volunteer work as the Ontario Director for ICROSS Canada, but he is also proud to have worked with other charities that make a difference; Health Partners International Canada, Feed the Children — Canada, "Sew-on-Fire" Ministry, Woman for Orphans & Widows (WOW!), Child Haven International, and Canadian Forces Personnel in Jamaica & Haiti.

"I am a little pencil in the hand of a writing God who is sending a love letter to the world."
Mother Teresa (birth name Agnes Gonxha Bojarhiu)

Mollie Colson was a typical tourist who loved to travel. In the year 2000 she accepted an invitation by her East African cousin Sheila, to 'safari' in Kenya and Tanzania. Like Billy and Lynn, Mollie looks back shaking her head at the life-changing events that followed.

Sheila dearly loved the Kenyan people and eagerly unveiled the beauties of Kenya — the wildlife and the cultural richness — to her guest. She also introduced Mollie to "the terrible other side." The impoverished and suffering, the sick and the dying children left a deep imprint on Mollie. She returned to Canada compelled to do something.

Coincidentally, a local newspaper article about ICROSS Canada caught her eye, and she did not hesitate to telephone the man named Billy Willbond to learn how she could contribute. Mollie began gathering items from friends and neighbours and getting the word out about the humanitarian organization. When Billy's email plea for knitters to make Izzy Comfort Dolls arrived in her inbox, she answered the call and organized a knitters' group called Mollie's Dollies. Touched by Mark Isfeld's story, Mollie even published The Dolls of Joy, a colourful and informative booklet about the Izzy Comfort Doll and ICROSS Canada. This booklet helped raise funds for ICROSS Canada's projects for the needy.

Mollie has traveled back to Africa with the Willbonds, not as a tourist but as a humanitarian messenger of peace delivering supplies and Izzy Dolls to some of the poorest on our planet. Her drop in the bucket, combined with the drops from the Willbonds and the other angels of ICROSS Canada, have become a small river of hope.

CHAPTER 6

MORE ANGELS FLY IN

THE NEW IZZY DOLL MAMA —
SHIRLEY O'CONNELL

"There seemed to be kids everywhere. I saw the devastation on their faces. I wanted to hug them. They should have something to hug. The Izzy Doll came into my mind. I don't know why because it wasn't connected at all, but it did!"

Shirley O'Connell's response to a TV broadcast of the
Tsunami disaster in Indonesia on Boxing Day 2004

Shirley O'Connell seems to smile even when she isn't. A devoted, warm, take-charge mom and grandmother, she is the archetype that Disney might choose for a family-themed movie. These qualities are no doubt why Carol Isfeld was convinced Shirley could take the helm as the new Izzy Doll Mama.

Shirley had read about the Izzy Doll story and the bronze statue in Calgary's Peacekeeper Park — a statue of a soldier giving an Izzy Doll to a child of war. She thought, "What a wonderful thing." But it wasn't until a few months later, Boxing Day 2004, that she thought of the dolls again. She remembers watching the shocking footage broadcast on television of the Tsunami disaster in Indonesia and thinking the children should have something to hug. The Izzy Doll popped into her mind.

Proficient at crocheting and knitting, making dolls for children to hug was something Shirley could do. She knew many other women would donate their time and talents to bring a smile to impoverished children too. A member of the Order of the Eastern Star (OES), a fraternal organization with chapters in every province but one, and 131 chapters in Ontario alone, she conceived the idea of taking the Izzy Doll project to the Eastern Star membership. Her plan was to take the story of the Izzy doll to the women who could make dolls, then coordinate doll pickups and liaise between military connections and aid organizations that were transporting the dolls to their destination.

She would also propose her plan to the Isfelds, strangers she had never met. Coincidently, Carol Isfeld was overwhelmed with worry at how to meet the number of dolls required. She had enlisted knitters, including family, friends, and women who had responded to the media stories about Mark and the Dolls. ICROSS knitters were also working diligently, yet Carol agonized over the fact that the need was greater than the current supply.

Shirley sought out the Isfelds' phone number and called. They talked, mother-to-mother, woman-to-woman, sister knitters with a desire to send dolls to children who would have something of their own to hug.

So began a relationship across the miles, Carol on Vancouver Island and Shirley in eastern Ontario. Although they would never actually meet they formed a close bond. Shirley came to

understand Carol very well, for they both had lost a loved one; Carol her son, and Shirley her husband. Both had found solace in their acts of goodwill to others, even through, or perhaps in spite of, their grief.

Carol considered Shirley an angel who arrived just in the nick of time with her talents and resources. Shirley was initially concerned about reproducing dolls exactly from the original Izzy pattern and suggested that perhaps knitters could use their own patterns. Carol agreed and eased Shirley's mind by telling her, "Don't worry what the dolls look like. No matter how it turns out, a little child will love it." In the language of their craft they discussed the patterns, adapting yarn colour that would best fit the child's culture and skin colour.

Born with a huge capacity for tenacity and tenderness, Shirley rallied women together. Her regular newsletters inspired members of the OES with the Izzy story, photos of children receiving the dolls, and the rising tallies of dolls created and distributed. She organized pickups of large batches of dolls from church groups, schools, senior centres, women's organizations, and knitting clubs. After sorting and packaging, the dolls are delivered to her military contact L Col (R) Ken Holmes, and to charities that include ICROSS Canada, HPIC, ORBIS, Child Haven International Canada and even some Shriner children's hospitals.

Delighted with Shirley's updates, emails, and phone calls, Carol spoke of the relief she now felt with such a substantial number of knitters to help meet the need for dolls.

Then one evening in August 2007 Shirley received a call from Brian with the news that Carol had been admitted to the hospital and was scheduled for surgery in the morning. Carol's premonitions were evident once again and she needed to ask Shirley if she would take on the role of the new Izzy Doll Mama.

"At the time I thought it was strange that Brian was calling me on behalf of Carol to ask such a question, because it never entered my head at first that she would not come out of the hospital. Both of us at times could be very intuitive, and as the evening wore on I just knew that she wasn't going to make it and that it was very important that she know that Mark's legacy would continue."

Shirley had humbly and wholeheartedly accepted. Carol's intuition was accurate; the request she had extended before passing through the veil between the here and the after would ensure the Izzy Doll project would continue. Brian said Carol was confident in Shirley's abilities and her devotion to the dolls. She believed that God had sent Shirley to take over as the new Izzy Doll Mama and she was at peace knowing the Izzy Doll project, so dear to her, was in good hands.

Shirley flew to Courtney B.C. for Carol's memorial service, where she met the Isfeld family, Carol's sister Judy, Brian's sister Pat, and a host of friends including me.

In the family home, Carol's presence could be felt. Her artwork hung on the walls and surrounded us like a spiritual gallery. Her ornamental angels and elephants dotted the mantles and shelves and seemed aware of the mourning in the room and that their owner was absent.

Carol loved everything and everyone in this room and I almost expected her to walk through the door with a tray of sandwiches and a big smile on her face.

A shelf in Carol's living room with angels of all kinds

Shirley sat on the same sofa where Carol had spent many hours crocheting, and Mikey curled up next to the new Izzy Doll Mamma, just as he had with Carol.

"I found it very, very difficult when Brian used the term New Izzy Doll Mama to describe me, and it really hit me hard when I was in their home prior to Carol's Memorial Service. They showed me the itinerary for the memorial, and there it was in black and white. I simply fell apart. There was no way I could ever fill Carol's shoes and the magnitude of what I had been asked to do overwhelmed me. I felt like a 'fake' and so unworthy of such an honour. What got me through those first few days was how important it was for the family that this incredible legacy of the Izzy Doll should continue."

As the Isfeld spokesperson, Leigh refers to Shirley warmly and with great respect as the new Izzy Doll Mama. Shirley admits, "It took me a long time to be comfortable in my new role and I truly hope that I have honoured Carol, Brian and Mark with my commitment and dedication to the Izzy Doll Program."

Shirley is handling the helm and her duties very well. And just as Carol recruited Shirley as her angel, Shirley, who also believes in angels, recruited some of her own. The bounty of dolls became so plenteous that provincial angels were enlisted. OES members Marion King and Betty Bush, as well as Sharon and Alex Whitehorne, are the provincial coordinators for Ontario. They ensure the pickup and delivery to Shirley's home in Perth, where the dolls are then sorted and earmarked for distribution.

OES members in other parts of Canada work diligently organizing dolls too: Sylvia McCleave in NS/PEI, Anne Murray in New Brunswick, Bernice Palmer in Quebec, Phyllis Dyck in Manitoba, Dorothy Mittelholtz in Saskatchewan, Barbara Prochnau in Alberta, and Dorene Bennie in BC/Yukon.

Along with the logistics of pickups and deliveries, Shirley makes presentations at schools, women's groups, and senior centres. Veterans Affairs Canada sponsors a program called Historica Encounters in Ottawa, which includes workshops for students from across Canada who attend Remembrance Week.

"At these workshops I still show the 'old' DVD that Brian made and then the students actually make their own Izzy Doll, which is then given to the military ... or to Major General Lewis MacKenzie for ICROSS Canada. The students receive just the knitted body of the doll and then they have to stuff it and sew it up. Both girls and boys participate."

The students discover the story of the Izzy Doll through Shirley's hands-on interactive presentations, and their comments after the event range from satisfaction to pride. As one student says, "What impacted me most was knowing that kids who aren't as fortunate as me can benefit so much from such a small contribution."

"Children are the well of the future" were Carol's profound words. For many of the students in this program it is the first time they have participated in a humanitarian cause, opening their minds to the plight of others and their hearts to do something about it.

Cass Dagg-Murphy and Shirley

THE PROJECT GROWS

"It's true that making Izzy Dolls helped Carol (and me) deal with the pain of losing our son. But neither Carol nor I expected the rush of enthusiasm that greeted – and still greets – the project."

Brian Isfeld

More and more people are attracted to the Izzy Doll story and the opportunity to use their talents to bring some measure of comfort to children in need. Shirley notes, "As of September 2011 members of the Order of the Eastern Star across Canada have collected and distributed more than 64,250 Izzy Dolls through the Canadian Military Engineers and other charitable organizations. ICROSS alone, since they started, have collected hundreds of thousands of Izzy Comfort Dolls. Doesn't it make you proud to be a Canadian?"

The Izzy Doll has an incredible effect on the crafters. The dolls arc the opposite of war and despair. In a world plagued with conflicts and bloodshed, making and giving an Izzy Doll is peace bestowed; a gesture of kindness. It was something purposeful for women of all ages and economic backgrounds; an easily affordable project that they felt was making a difference. The Izzy Doll has become the expression of hope and a symbol of mothers' love. Hundreds of Izzy Doll creators would echo what Shirley had reasoned when she first learned about the dolls, that it was "something I could do." A witness to the power of a little ball of yarn personified, Shirley affirms, "The Izzy Doll speaks on behalf of Canadian Women."

With almost five years experience with the Izzy Doll project, Shirley reflects on the future of the dolls this way:

"At times I have wondered how long Canadian women and girls will continue to knit the dolls, and it certainly has been a concern over the past couple of years as to how I can manage to send the dolls overseas since the Department of National Defence changed their policy to exclude 'humanitarian' items from going to Afghanistan because of the danger to our soldiers and the children. However, God works in strange ways, and thanks to ICROSS Canada who have allowed me to distribute dolls through their system of charity organizations, the little, truly Canadian Izzy Doll still manages to bring smiles to the less fortunate children.

So the bottom line is, as long as these beautiful little Izzy Dolls continue to arrive at my door, and as long as I can continue to find ways of getting them out of Canada and overseas to the little children, I will continue accepting them. The payback can never be measured, it is a gift from God and I feel I have been truly blessed to have been given this opportunity."

Shirley O'Connell and Canadian Army Veteran Tim McCully, who is involved with the CAV Motorcycle Unit that fundraises and collects Izzy Dolls around Ontario, were presented with the ICROSS Canada Humanitarian Award on May 2, 2010, at CFB Kingston.

Just as the knitters were foremost in Carol's mind, when Shirley heard she would receive the ICROSS Canada Humanitarian Award her first thoughts were for the women she called devoted knitters. "This comes as a complete surprise and I will look forward to sharing this award with all the many women who have knitted their little hearts out to make so many Izzy Dolls for the children around the world."

Carol could not have known that Mark's initial request for something for the children would have become a Canadian phenomenon with such a global impact. What she did understand was that the Izzy Doll project was a joint undertaking that flourished, based on the tenet of strength in numbers. Her gratitude and thankfulness flowed freely to her "angels"

Hi Dearest Helpers!

"First I have to thank God, I really needed help to see that Mark got something to help him. Then when the idea came from his 'Doll Picture' I worked on how, and after many trials and measurements 'I got it.' He was so, so happy, he could sleep remembering smiles! His sapper buddies loved it and teased him. On my birthday June 2, 1994, his last call to me, he said 'the dolls are a hit Mom, please keep making them.' How could I not! He was gone and I needed control again! His buddies needed them (Izzy Dolls) to get Mark's feeling and so many people needed my feeling of 'doing something!' Then one day I just sat down and bawled, I couldn't keep it up. Only one me and so, so, many kids. I needed helpers.

I again asked God to help. Then with Brian's help on the computer, and being the Silver Cross Mother, it was televised and my helpers started. Thanks to people like you it's never stopped. Billy Willbond and all his helpers make Izzy Comfort Dolls, so I feel so grateful, so thankful to you all.

God Bless You All - All - Ways - Carol"

Ethel Ryckman, Maureen McTavish, Sharon Barefoot Didsbury AB Hospital Auxilary

St Martin's Anglican Church Calgary

The text on this page is arranged in the shape of a lit candle.

Billy says not to forget the Catholic Women League Knitters, the Anglican Church Knitters, the United Church Knitters and the Baptist Church Knitters in all provinces and territoriesof our Country

Orchard View Living Centre KnittersHooks & Needles Guild Northumberland , Carlton House Victoria. Colchester County knitters Nova Scotia, St. Andrews United Church Truro, N.S. There is Mrs. Hyatt, a widow from Nova Scotia who knits a box of dolls every week. Ann Scott who has knit more than 2000 dolls herself since she began knitting Izzy Dolls in 2006. There are hundreds of individual knitters like Marg Irvine of Vancouver and Vivian Brooke Harte of Victoria, both examples of ladies over 80 years of age who knit up a storm. And there is Queenie Mills from Manitoba who is 93...

The Knitting Circle of Hickory Wits , Knitters, Top U.C.W, Northshore Pins & Needles Castor Valley Elementary School, Caroline Residence Group, Chartwell O.E.S., The 163 Nottawasag Matthews Churc Ont,

Hills- or the Gloucester Senior Generation Club Knitters, The Durward Quilters (knitters), Bloordale, Quilting & Stitchery Guild, Lanark County Knitting Guild, Bloordale, U.C.W, Loyal Chapter # 76, O.E.S., Suites, Perth, Riverside Anglican/United Church, Ottawa Ladies Kanata Retirement Residence Knitters, McDonald Chapter, LA Knitters, Knitting Guild of Chattanooga Tennessee, a Handweavers & Spinners Guild, Circle of Friends, St. Anglican Church, Stonehaven Manor Knitters, St. Paul's United h, Perth, Hands In Mission, First Baptist Church, Tillsonburg, Atikokan Ladies Knitting Group, Knitty Nods of Brantford, Garth Trails Izzy Doll'rs, Knit Wits Angus, Ontario, Hands Touching Hearts (New Jersey Knitting Group), Mount Carmel Mission Group Knitters, United Church Knitters, Tottenham Woman's Group, CWl Knitters, Didsbury Hospital Auxiliary, 'Mollie Dollies' group on Galiano Island & the -We Gulf Islanders Love To Do Crafts. The Knitwits of Meadowbrook on Salt Spring Island, St. Martin's Anglican Church Knitters Group, Calgary, Knitters from Uptown Yarns, Courtenay, Knitters from Village Yarn Shoppe, Comox. Mount Carmel Mission Group Knitters, Eastern Star Group Knitters, Knitters from Village Yarn Shoppe, Comox. Knitters from Uptown Yarns Courtenay, the Waterford Residence, Barrie Ontario, Didsbury Hospital Auxiliary, and many, many more...

Knit Adults' Centre

CHAPTER 7

LANDMINES: "THE COWARDLY SOLDIER"

In a chain of events pertaining to Mark's life, people have been drawn into the story and have become key players for positive change. Major General John Arch MacInnis led the subsequent inquiry conducted after Mark was killed. The Maj General was so moved by what he had learned about landmines that upon his retirement he committed to the new role of Director of the United Nations Mine Action Service, developing a set of standards that "provides for the protection of deminers all around the world."

ANTI-PERSONNEL LANDMINES FACT SHEET

"Vision without action is just a dream; action without vision is passing the time; but vision with action can change the world."

Nelson Mandela

Landmine estimate: Some reports suggest that between 45 and 50 million landmines are still in the ground in at least 70 countries. It is reported that landmines maim or kill 10,000 civilians every year."

Landmine casualties: There are approximately 6,000 new casualties each year globally — as opposed to the 25,000 annual rate recorded in the late 1990s.

The death toll continues: In Somalia, between 2008 and 2009, 93 children were killed by landmines. Twenty-four types of anti-personnel mines from 10 different countries have been identified. No minefield records were kept. http://warvictims.wordpress.com

Iron Harvest: This is the name given to the ordnance that has been hauled away after being ploughed up from farmers' fields in Belgium and France every year since WWI. Large quantities of munitions still remain a danger, buried in the fields of the former battlegrounds of Europe and Asia.

Adopt-A-Minefield Campaign 1999-2009: The Canadian Landmine Foundation was a founding partner of this ten-year global campaign. Canadians funded $3,700,000 for mine action projects that cleared more than two million square metres, assisted survivors, and financed the training of canine detection dogs. Worldwide, the campaign raised over $25 million, cleared 1,000 minefields, destroyed more than 44 million mines, in fourteen countries, and supported thousands of landmine survivors.

The Ottawa Treaty: Also called the Anti-Personnel Mine Ban Convention, this treaty was signed December 3, 1997. Signing countries, or states parties, agreed to ban the production, use, and trade of anti-personnel landmines. They also committed to eliminate their stockpiles of landmines within four years of ratifying the agreement and to actively seek out and remove the landmines from their land within ten years. As of August 2011, 156 countries have signed the Anti-Personnel Mine Ban. Thirty-seven states have not signed, including China, India, Pakistan, Russia and the United States.

Countries now mine-free: As of December 2009, fifteen countries participating in the Ottawa Treaty have been cleared and declared mine-free: Nigeria, Bulgaria, Costa Rica, El Salvador, France, Guatemala, Honduras, FYR Macedonia, Malawi, Suriname, Swaziland, Albania, Greece, Rwanda, and Zambia.

A WORLD PROBLEM

"Once peace is declared the landmine does not recognize that peace. The landmine is eternally prepared to take victims."
Jody Williams, coordinator of the International Campaign to Ban Landmines
and Nobel Peace Prize laureate

My hands are immersed in hot sudsy water, washing the supper dishes at the sink. I'm deep in thought, trying to process all the unbelievable stories and information I've been learning about landmines. The kitchen window is wide open inviting in the sweet aroma of a barbecue two doors down. I'm watching the kids romp across the lawns and sidewalks, giggling and singing. These sights and sounds are synonymous with a Canadian summer afternoon; they make me smile. Then my memory jolts, shifting gears from this placid setting to a tragedy in a meadow in the former Yugoslavia in 2000. It is a true story that reminds me of the importance of de-miners like Mark Isfeld. It was told to me by Scott Fairweather of the Canadian Landmine Foundation.

Eleven year-old Ema Alic and her two friends were playing in a meadow, near Sarajevo, Bosnia. They were happily absorbed in their own world of childhood games, unaware of the menace hiding beneath the tall grass. It was an anti-personnel mine, a compact device of wire and metal, waiting to perform its intended purpose of injuring and maiming. A remnant of bitter conflict, it wasn't programmed to know that war had ended five years previously, nor could it know the difference between the footstep of an ally, an enemy, or an innocent child. It simply reacts.

The explosion fractured the silence of that April afternoon. Ema's parents and neighbours recognized the all too familiar sound, foreboding chaos and carnage. Filled with terror, they rushed to the edge of the meadow but went no farther. Terrified to run into a minefield where more landmines may lay in wait to ambush, they stood paralyzed. Ema's two friends died right away, but Ema was still alive. The agonizing screams of their daughter ripped at their hearts. For several hours they watched at a distance unable to reach out to aid and comfort. A mine clearance team arrived eventually but by then Ema was dead. It was an unconscionable scene because it could have been prevented. Later reports revealed that although this patch of land was scheduled for mine clearing it did not happen because of lack of funding.

Still at the kitchen sink, I'm now scouring the skillet with excess vigour. The frying pan is taking the brunt of the anger and repugnance I feel for these anti-personnel weapons invented and utilized solely to cause pain and suffering. Military strategists in the throes of war would call the casualties "necessary collateral damage" meant to tie up their adversarys' energy, distract them, and drain their resources. I have contempt for the warlords, insurgents, and military leaders who cannot clean up after themselves and who lack the foresight of a future after their conflict ends. And all conflicts end eventually.

I live in a country free of landmines. I was ignorant to this world problem until Brian and Carol acquainted me with the details and the profound seriousness of this issue. Not only did a landmine take their son's life, landmines continue to wreak havoc by maiming and killing people and animals and rendering valuable land useless.

Landmines are indiscriminate. It is not uncommon for a curious child to pick up a landmine as though it was a treasure — a surprise nestled in a clump of grass or poking out between reeds in a stream. And it is all too common for an unsuspecting farmer, traveler or tourist to trigger a mine lurking just under the soil, leaving the victim crippled, blind, or dead. Cattle, sheep, and wildlife, including endangered species, are just as often innocent victims.

As well as jeopardizing lives, anti-personnel mines have a lasting effect on the economy. Land condemned as impassable lies untouched, thus restricting the community's access to viable areas, water sources, and food. Resettlement, agriculture, tourism, and development are stunted for decades, affecting the community's ability to rebuild. The flow of relief apportioned to post-war areas is impeded when aid workers traveling mined roads and terrain are injured or killed.

Even more barbaric is the fact that many of the warring factions do not keep accurate records, or any records at all that could ensure landmine removal after a conflict. So it remains a brutal game of hide and seek with devastating consequences.

Ema's story makes me question how a community could possibly have 'peace' when the memories of the past constantly erupt under their feet. How can a population ever resettle, rebuild, and resume normal lives when gloom and doom lurk in their midst?

Jody Williams and Carol

AMBIGUOUS PEACE

"Peace, in the sense of the absence of war, is of little value to someone who is dying of hunger or cold. It will not remove the pain of torture inflicted on a prisoner of conscience. It does not comfort those who have lost their loved ones in floods caused by senseless deforestation in a neighbouring country. Peace can only last where human rights are respected, where people are fed, and where individuals and nations are free."

The XIVth Dalai Lama

While I'm still at the kitchen window, my five-year-old grandson catches my attention. Trying to master the finesse of using his brakes, he falls off his bright red bicycle. His mother runs to his side and hugs him. She wipes his tears; his sobbing abates. He is once again up and riding toward the grassy park with his mother running beside him to help him balance. They are free — unhindered by the fear of deadly landmines hidden under the ground laying in wait. That wasn't so for Ema's parents or for millions of parents in war-torn countries who wish for freedom from fear.

I am tempted to take the Pollyanna view that all countries live in peace and freedom after war ends, but that would be presumptuous because each country's circumstance is so different. I wonder then, what is the meaning of peace. An old vet once told me that peace meant an absence of war. In Bosnia on the day Ema and her friends were killed, war was long over — so that definition held no water.

Here is another claim to the real meaning of peace by an unknown author: "Peace does not mean to be in a place where there is no noise, trouble, or hard work. Peace means to be in the midst of all those things and still be calm in your heart. That is the real meaning of peace."

This is a lovely spiritual quote, but for me, as a mother, it seems impractical and incomplete especially as I recall another incident in 2007. Six children in Mozambique, who were all siblings, found an explosive device, a leftover from a sixteen-year civil war. They tried to open it and were killed in the ensuing explosion. I cannot imagine the emotional state of the parents after losing their six children. It seems humanly impossible to be "calm in your heart" after such an unbearable tragedy. It is beyond comprehension.

Now here is a definition that speaks to me: "Peace is not something you wish for: it's something you make, something you do, something you are, and something you give away." This piece of wisdom is from Robert Fulghum, American sage and author of *All I Really Need to Know I Learned in Kindergarten* published in 1988.

Canadians generally like to think we are a peaceful nation with hopes for a peaceful world. But hope and wishing are not enough. According to Fulghum's definition, peace is an action; making, doing, being and giving.

There is proof that Canadians have been in the mood and are active for peace. Canada's Lester B. Pearson was awarded the Nobel Peace Prize in 1957 for organizing the United Nations Emergency Force. He is considered the founder of the concept of diffusing conflict with a neutral force; a force eventually called Peacekeepers.

In the sixties, Canada experienced unprecedented growth and economic prosperity. Within the context of a changing country, a new citizenry slowly emerged. Humanitarian agencies delivered messages on TV showing footage of starving children a continent away that elicited the compassion of Canadians feeling blessed by their own affluence.

Donations and volunteer hours increased with every decade and people were finding creative ways besides writing a cheque, to contribute their philanthropy. Skilled professionals such as dentists and eye doctors have set up free clinics for the destitute in inner-cities around the world. Their assistants volunteer and pay their own transportation and room and board for the opportunity to serve the needy.

Even vacationing has taken on a humanitarian twist, with Canadian tourists packing school supplies or toys for the poor in the tropical countries they visit.

Many Canadians are aware of their responsibility as global citizens. Soldiers like Mark felt this way too. He was deployed on three United Nations Peacekeeping missions, saw the casualties of landmine explosions, and understood the hazards of his chosen career. Proud of the fact that Canada and 1CER could provide their skills to bring a climate of peace, he said in one of his letters, *"We think about the lives we save but not the one we risk."* He repeatedly said he was making a difference. Mark knew what Peacekeeping was all about. He felt it. He acted on it. He gave his life for it. It was not about accolades and awards. He knew Peacekeepers were risking their lives so others could have life. It was all about doing, making, being, and giving for Peace! And Mark's parents told his story proudly, in the hope of inspiring others to take action for the same peace.

WORKING TOGETHER

Never doubt that a small group of thoughtful, committed people can change the world. Indeed, it is the only thing that ever has.

Cultural anthropologist, Margaret Meade

Brian and Carol Isfeld knew little of the horrific consequences of anti-personnel mines prior to Mark's accident. But from that moment on they committed to avenues of action to ban landmines and save lives.

They met with the people from Mine Action Canada (MAC) and were impressed with the committment of this organization. Their attitude prompted Brian's praise that they were "the most dedicated and caring people in the world."

MAC believes eliminating disasters caused by landmines and post-war weapons is solvable and possible within our lifetime. This organization works in conjunction with international partners to make its theory a reality.

The Canadian Landmine Foundation (CLMF) is another organization that works to raise awareness of landmines. It also raises funds for mine removal and for the support of landmine victims. Carol and Brian joined CLMF in the hope of making a difference.

As stated by the Canadian Landmine Foundation, "Landmine victims suffer debilitating physical and emotional injuries, victims' families and communities are plagued by psychological and economic burdens, and the environmental impact of landmines on their surroundings is significant. Landmines also impede long-term reconstruction of war-torn societies, the return of refugees and internally displaced persons to their homes, and political reconciliation and peace."

People of post-war countries often lack the resources to meet the need for medical services, prosthetics, and job opportunities and training for the victims disabled by landmines. As a result, the life of an amputee remains in a constant state of survival. Wheelchairs and crutches can be unaffordable, restricting mobility and reducing the individual to the life of a shut-in, and when the sole breadwinner is maimed or killed the whole family is profoundly affected, often ensuring a life of abject poverty.

Two men, survivors of landmine accidents, realized the need for a network of cooperation and formed the Landmine Survivor Network or LSN. This network of support of people helping people, has become a humanitarian force for peace.

In 1984 while camping in the Golan Heights, twenty-year-old Jerry White stepped on a landmine. He lost his right foot. Ken Rutherford was working for the International Rescue Committee in Somalia when his jeep hit a landmine. He lost both of his legs.

After recovering from their personal traumatic encounters and while traveling to garner support for a landmine ban, Jerry and Ken met. Each had witnessed the disturbing lack of services and aid for landmine victims, mostly in third world countries and they knew there was a lot to be done.

Even the name, Landmine Survivor Network, elevates individuals to a place of empowerment and hope as survivors not victims. The LSN works with more than 180 agencies and governments setting up an infrastructure that can address the needs of landmine survivors in the areas of health, economic opportunities, and human rights. Utilizing peer counselling, amputee survivors are matched with field workers who have had similar traumatic experiences. Forming a relationship of genuine understanding, they can educate others about the resources available. LSN has made approximately 100,000 visits through their peer program, enabling survivors to become self- sustainable and live life more fully.

Brian joined the Landmine Survivor's Network and became their Canadian delegate. He believed that victims need not lose hope. With support, encouragement and concrete help, they could become survivors.

THE OTTAWA TREATY

"Thousands and many more in years to come will owe their lives and limbs to this intelligent, compassionate and effective initiative."

John Kenneth Galbraith, Canadian Landmine Foundation website

On December 3, 1997, in Ottawa, Carol and Brian Isfeld attended what Brian reported as, "the largest international conference ever held in Canada and maybe the most important one to many, many people worldwide."

The purpose of the conference was the signing of a landmine ban treaty described by Brian as "the beginning of the end of a horrendous and wicked weapon of war." The Ottawa Treaty was the result of the leadership of the Canadian Government working in conjunction with international organizations and the International Campaign to Ban Landmines (ICBL). It was a momentous signing with a timeline aimed at clearing huge areas of land and financially supporting landmine survivors. After the signing of the Ottawa Treaty, Scott Fairweather remarked:

"This treaty marks the first time in the history of the world that civil society and government have come together to eliminate a weapon that has some military use, because it impacts on civilians. And it was developed at the urging of the Government of Canada, led by then Foreign Affairs Minister Lloyd Axworthy, who now serves on the Canadian Landmine Foundation Board."

Jody Williams, ICBL founding coordinator, and the ICBL were awarded the 1997 Nobel Peace Prize for their efforts to bring about the Ottawa Treaty; a landmine ban to cease the making, selling, and use of anti-personnel landmines.

To Brian, addressing the conference on behalf of the Landmine Survivors was a great responsibility. It was a full house that included VIPs such as Prime Minister Chrétien and the Secretary General of the United Nations, Kofi Annan.

Although he liked to appear stoic, Brian commented that it was a relief Lloyd Axworthy was positioned right behind him in case he should fall over while delivering his message. Carol said Brian did well and that he had even managed to bring then Deputy Prime Minister Sheila Copps to tears, which, in Brian's opinion, was a tough task.

In his speech Brian emphasized the difference between the victims and the survivors of landmine accidents. Mark was a victim who lost his life. Those faced with either the loss of a loved one or an injury are the survivors, who must find a way to carry on. He emphasized that it is their needs that must be addressed.

"The amazing fact is that we can do something about the problem. And we are doing something, collectively, in concert with people from many nations. But the signature on the document does not signal the end of the problem. Indeed it is only the beginning, for we must now address the enormous cost both financially and in human suffering caused by these weapons of terror. We can stop making and selling and using mines, but if we leave them in the ground dispersed around the globe, what are the consequences to those who must live in proximity with them? We must accelerate efforts to de-mine the globe conscientiously. We must address the rehabilitation and return to gainful employment of the thousands of mine victims world wide, else the treaty signing will prove to be an empty gesture."

Brian spoke of his son as a fiercely proud Canadian who wore his uniform with pride and of the devastating effect Mark's death had had on his family. And he concluded with his own words of patriotism and a final plea:

"But as Canadians, we must make that little extra effort in support and encouragement of our own military and civilian de-miners; we must support our humanitarian workers in the field and at home; and we must give all possible support to world wide landmine victims, ensuring they become landmine survivors. That is the Canadian Way. There can be no other way."

At this conference Brian and Carol were introduced to landmine survivors in attendance. Carol had said that their positive outlook and their courage to push for world change inspired her and Brian. Here are a few of their personal stories, paraphrased from Brian's writings:

Kong Chim, a Cambodian, was out collecting firewood near her home when she stepped on a landmine. The young girl lost her leg. Entry into a skills training program enabled Chim to become a tailor, which led to her teaching other landmine survivors to make a living through the creation of fine handicrafts.

Kong Chim

Usman Fitrat, an Afghani boy of eleven, picked up a mine. It exploded severing both hands and blinding him. Less than two weeks earlier a mine had killed his mother and cousin.

Marianne Holtz, from Idaho, U.S.A., was working as a nurse for the American Refugee Committee near Goma, Zaire, when the truck she was riding in hit a landmine. She lost both legs below the knees, broke her back, and sustained facial damage. The landmine that almost killed her cost a mere $3 but caused almost half a million dollars of medical and related expenses. Marianne is an advocate for the Survivors Corps.

Kamel Sa'adi lost his left leg to a landmine while picnicking with friends near the Jordon / Israeli border. He was fourteen at the time. Now an adult, Kamel helps landmine survivors through a Jordanian non-profit organization he founded in 2007 called Life Line Consultancy and Rehabilitation.

Chris Moon is admired by people from all walks of life. While clearing mines in Mozambique, this young man from the UK stepped on an explosive device that took his lower right leg and right arm. Less than a year after the accident he was competing in the London Marathon and has since competed in dozens of races, raising hundreds of thousands of dollars for prosthetics for landmine victims and for charities for the disabled. He has climbed mountains, trekked across the Australian outback, and completed his Masters degree in Security Management. Chris continues to inspire through his book *One Step Beyond*, and as an international speaker.

Brian and Chris Moon

Tun Channareth: Tun was born in Phnom Penh and grew up under cruel regimes during tumultuous times. While on a mission as a resistance soldier in 1982 he stepped on a landmine. It cost him both legs. Seeing a future of limitation and hopelessness, he had thought about ending his life. After years of vocational training, Tun began making wheelchairs for landmine survivors, an occupation that provided an income for his family. He quickly became engulfed in the pain and loss of other survivors. His empathy for them and their families propelled him to became a force for change and a vital member of ICBL. In fact he was chosen to accept the 1997 Nobel Peace Prize on behalf of this community. He delivered a moving speech describing the producers, exporters, and governments that make landmines as "architects of death and destruction" who use their skill and energy to "find new ways of blowing one another apart and killing peace."

Tun spoke of the alliance that he had been forged between him and three veterans of a past war. Now as fellow amputees they shared a common goal. "Before, we were soldiers of four rival armies that laid mines that blew the legs and arms off one another." Now Tun says they have become allies and "We beg the world to stop making mines. We beg the world to stop laying mines. We beg the world to give money for demining and development so that we can rebuild our lives, our communities, our villages, and our countries again!"

Tun made strong arguments for why landmines should not be manufactured in the first place. It was obvious that countries who resist joining the landmine ban continue to profit from the manufacturing and sales of landmines and it bothered Tun. He explained how compassion gave him the power to persevere:

"Each day I go with a friend, Hul Bros, to visit others injured by mines or polio in Siem Reap. We travel up to 40 kilometres a day on a motorbike — one leg between two of us! When I met these villagers without rice, without limbs, some without hope, my heart is touched. Children injured by landmines bring tears to my eyes. These new friends are precious gifts, sacraments. They draw out mercy and compassion from me. Without them this metta-karuna (loving kindness) might be still locked inside and I would not know the power it has to urge me to change evil into good."

He spoke of landmines as a metaphor for the landmines of the heart, which lie in all of us and he encourages us all to be strong and work together: "If we ban the landmines of the heart along with the landmines in the earth, the needs of the poor will take priority over the wants of the rich; the freedom of the dominated over the liberty of the powerful, and marginalized groups will be included. Together we can stop a coward's war that makes victims of us all."

Author's Note: A number of years ago LSN changed its name to Survivors Corp. During their thirteen years they have changed laws and practices to accommodate the needs of landmine survivors and have improved the lives of those who would otherwise be forgotten. More recently, Jerry White and the Board of Directors decentralized the work of LSN passing the torch to the many NGOs in place to continue their work.

A SUCCESS STORY

"The eradication of anti-personnel mines around the world is one of the most important tasks facing the international community."

Norman Jewison, Honorary Director, Canadian Landmine Foundation

Hamad is a young boy who lives with his family on Bibi Mahro hill in Kabul, Afghanistan. His comments about life before and after demining are recorded in an interview found in the 1384 Progress Report of Mine Action Programme for Afghanistan (MAPA).

"Many times we saw cows and dogs what (sic) were blown up by the mines that lay around our house … one of my next door neighbours also lost his leg to a mine on the hill." Referring to 2002, when MAPA cleared the Bibi Mahro hill of UXO, Hamad said, "After the destruction of 37 ATMs, (anti-tank mine) 2,151 APMs (anti-personnel mine) and 6,133 pieces of UXO, (Unexploded Ordnance), Bibi Mahro was declared clear and safe. … People are coming to our hills to see the beautiful view of Kabul. Now children can play."

Hamad's friend Ahmad was inspired by the skilled Sappers. He said, "These de-miners are better than heroes …They are playing with their lives to save other's lives. If I could be a de-miner I would, because it would serve my country. I want my country to be rebuilt."

THE TOUCH OF CELEBRITY

"Imagine the war is finished and you go to work and there are snipers shooting at you. Imagine taking your kids to the beach and you find that the beach is blowing up beneath you. Like there's nowhere safe. That's what I think is insidious about landmines and that's why I support Adopt-A-Minefield."

Sir Paul McCartney, Patron of Adopt-A-Minefield

One of the annual follow-up meetings on the progress of the Ottawa Treaty and the states parties was held in Geneva, Switzerland, in 2000. The Isfelds attended, sitting in on presentations and hearing the updated reports.

The participation of celebrities has helped to bring attention to the landmine issue. A personal highlight for Carol was meeting Heather Mills and her then husband Sir Paul McCartney, who was Carol's 1960's era teenage idol. Their celebrity profile was another boost to raise world awareness of the human suffering caused by anti-personal landmines. Carol presented them with an Izzy Doll signifying the Isfelds' recognition and gratitude for Paul and Heather's work in the service of peace.

Carol was also pleased to be able to present Izzy Dolls to landmine survivors who attended the conference. She said these people were the real heroes and that it was their experiences and their voices that were most profound.

DIANA – ADVOCATE FOR LANDMINE SURVIVORS

"I am a humanitarian, not a political figure. All I am trying to do is help. I am trying to highlight a problem that is going on all around the world."

Diana, Princess of Wales

Diana, Princess of Wales was a generous advocate for landmine survivors and supported the landmine ban. Her high profile brought mass attention to the cause, particularly to the injuries and deaths of children. In 1997 she visited Angola, where between ten and twenty million mines deployed during the 27-year-long civil war still hid beneath the soil. In August of the same year co-founders Jerry White and Ken Rutherford of the Landmine Survivors Network (now known as Survivor Corps) escorted Princess Diana on her last humanitarian mission to Bosnia-Herzegovina to meet landmine survivors.

In appreciation of the Princess' active participation in the landmine ban cause, Carol and Brian sent her an Izzy Doll and a note of gratitude. She responded:

I wanted to write to you personally, as I was so touched by your very moving letter. As a mother myself, I cannot begin to imagine your heartache of having lost your wonderful son, who was obviously so brave and dedicated. I truly believe anyone who undertakes the horrendous task of demining, must indeed be a very special and courageous person.

For my part, I am extremely grateful that I have been given the opportunity to help, in some way, to highlight the horror of these dreadful weapons. I have received many, many letters of support from all over the world and, with this encouragement, I shall carry on fighting this cause, striving for a worldwide ban and for continued support for the victims, those who care for them and their families and also for those de-mining the land.

I too, have great admiration for Chris Moon who is a shining example to us all, of inner strength and sheer determination to stop this totally unnecessary suffering. With my best wishes,

Yours Sincerely,

Diana

Angelina Jolie and Brad Pitt are examples of celebrities who continue to generously donate their name, their time and funding toward raising landmine awareness.

CANINE HELP

"of all our dreams today there is none more important or so hard to realize than that of peace in the world. May we never lose our faith in it or our resolve to do everything that can be done to convert it one day into reality."

Lester B. Pearson

In 2003, the CLMF announced that a 27,000 square mile area of land in Bila Vilka, Croatia, would be demined in MCpl Mark Isfeld's name, freeing roads and land for travel and development. The chosen location was near where Mark had lost his life demining (Kakma, Croatia) in 1994. From his mother's point of view, this tribute recognized her son's desire for peace. Carol commented about this honour, "It was just another way that Mark is still working. He would be so proud."

The cost of demining an area this size, approximately $67,000, was made possible through the Peacekeeper's De-mining Fund and individual donations to CLMF.

The CLMF also began funding the training of mine detection dogs (MDD) with Canadian International De-mining Corps (CIDC). Using canines was a strategy Brian had called for after Mark's death. He said he was satisfied to hear that dogs would now be employed and soldiers' lives saved.

Currently there are seventeen CLMF-funded mine detection dogs in training or deployed in Bosnia-Herzegovina, Croatia, and Afghanistan. Dogs had been used for clearing explosive devices after WWII but have gained more widespread acceptance in the last decade. Their keen sense of smell, matched with their intelligence and ability to work well with humans, has established man's best friend as an amazing ally in the de-mining process.

Most of the dogs in the CLMF canine de-mine program are German Shepherds. Working as a team with their handlers, they sniff out an explosive charge without actually coming in contact with it. Their rate of effectiveness is ten times that of a human team. The safety and due care for these loyal dogs is of utmost importance to the CIDC and CLF, and they are proud of the fact that, "There has not been a Canadian-trained MDD killed or injured in the field." (CLMF Website.)

Three canines named Izzy, Carol, and Brian are currently working together in Bosnia and Herzegovina clearing mines, saving lives, and continuing the task of making peace in the once war-torn land. Three dogs named Paul (after Cpl. Paul Davis), Jeff (after Master Cpl. Jeffrey Walsh) and Boomer (after Cpl. Andrew Eykelenboom) are currently working in Southern Afghanistan.

THERE IS HOPE IN ACTION

"The statistics of mines that need clearance are staggering but the truth is it's a challenge that is absolutely doable."

David Knopfler, Scottish singer/songwriter

At the time the Isfelds became active in the landmine action, there were so many landmines lurking in the soil that no one could even venture a guess at the number. After joining the movement they saw the count quantified and termed "finite." Although progress has been made, the estimates are still daunting and are predictors of catastrophe waiting to happen. But there is hope in continued action.

The Ottawa Treaty was the impetus for the success of the clearing of millions of acres. This action was the result of civilians and governments uniting to bring change.

At the 2004 States Parties conference in Nairobi, Kenya, Guy Willoughby, director of The HALO Trust, questioned why the international community is nowhere near where it should be in eliminating landmines. "Why is the work not finished?… Probably because the senior managers think landmines must be treated like other humanitarian disasters and need a full blown 'multi-layered' response, like the responses for drought, flooding, hurricanes, locust or HIV AIDS. But these are all recurring — mines are not. The lucky thing is that MINES DON'T HAVE SEX. Once cleared, mines are gone, finito, terminado, khallas."

Mr. Willoughby followed his question with a plea for "a commitment to intensify and accelerate our mine clearance efforts." Many years have gone by since the conference and Guy Willoughby's criticism is still relevant today.

The world is finally awake to landmine issues, but every mine that remains in the ground is an accident waiting to happen. Brian said it succinctly; "We can do something, we are doing something, but we must not become complacent. There is still too much work to do."

Author's Note: The cost of running mine clearing programs is both a commitment of man-hours and dollars. In the last few years the Canadian Landmine Foundation has had to adapt to these costs. In a 2011 email update, Scott Fairweather wrote: "CLMF is not gone — I laid myself and my colleague off so that the Foundation could be preserved. I still volunteer and, in fact, am working with the Board to organise a fundraiser in Toronto this November — we hope to raise over $40,000 and are planning to do a clearance in Mozambique and a mine risk education project for children in Afghanistan. In fact, a recent Board member (actually over a year now) is Wendy Hayward, mother of Cpl. James Hayward Arnal who was killed by an Improvised Explosive Device (IED) while on a foot patrol in Panjwayi District, Afghanistan, on July 18, 2008. The work is, of course, harder without fulltime staff."

CHAPTER 8

IN THE MOOD FOR PEACE: THE STORY OF THE IZZY DOLL

Unlike the hard, iron skeleton of war, the Izzy doll is soft and cuddly. Not forced upon, it is given freely and accepted easily. It cannot be bought or sold therefore has no monetary power. It is created in the spirit of love and given in the same. A gesture of kindness, it brings hope to those who have lost hope. It is created by, and distributed by volunteers, all who are in the mood for peace. In a world full of woes and wrongs, it is cheerful and right...And it is a gift of peace.

My observation of the Izzy Doll, Phyllis

THE CHARISMA OF THE IZZY DOLL

Marion King sat patiently at the Pearson Airport waiting for her flight number to be called. She began a conversation with a fellow traveler next to her. It was soon revealed that Marion was a member of the Order of the Eastern Star and makes Izzy Dolls. He was a service man in the Canadian military, and has given Izzy Dolls to children of war. They are instant friends.

The Izzy Doll story is a love story that began with a mother's gift to ease her child's burden as he helped the children. (At the time her son was over thirty years of age, but as the saying goes, "once a mother; always a mother.")

It was difficult for Mark Isfeld to see children who didn't have even basic necessities, a sense of safety, or a real childhood. It was such a contrast to the lives of Canadian children with their overflowing toy boxes, balanced meals, music lessons, and organized sports. Mark and his mother both knew a doll could not end war, feed the starving, or heal the ailing body. But giving a toy to play with was something they could do, and it was something important.

Play is natural and vital for the healthy development of a child, and toys are the tools for learning. In particular, a doll can be the object of a child's affection and the opportunity to model motherhood. A doll can be a friend to talk to, a personal confidante who can help relieve stress in chaotic times. A doll can ignite the imagination and transport the traveler into fantasyland, and that can be a saving grace for a child living in a war zone or in the depths of poverty.

For some children the Izzy Doll is their only toy, and for the poorest of the poor it is likely their only worldly possession. For those who die young it is the companion they clutch as they cross over into death. And for those who survive into adulthood, their doll is a reminder of a country that sent aid and medicines that likely improved conditions and their chance for survival.

The phenomenon of the Izzy doll is not only about the sheer number of dolls created. It is also about the momentum of wills that snowballed to produce something great. After Mark's death, 1CER kept the project going with their benevolent request to continue distributing the dolls. The media spread the story from coast to coast via television, radio, and newsprint, inspiring knitting groups and individuals. ICROSS Canada, and Shirley, and the OES collaborated with women nationwide to fill the demand. More volunteers cheerfully organized and loaded the boxes readying the shipment for its voyage.

When the dolls arrive at their destination they are distributed by aids, nurses, clergy, teachers, and soldiers. Correspondance from the field describe the big smiles on the faces of everyone as they distribute the dolls to outstretched hands of the delighted children.

With every mile of the Izzy Doll's journey the message of peace rings louder and clearer. Not just a doll but a presence; a ball of yarn that had somehow morphed into a marvellous miracle of goodwill and cheer. The momentum continues to grow; the Izzy Doll project that burgeoned from Carol Isfeld's living room spreads right across Canada.

If there is one thing to be learned from the Izzy Doll project, it is strength in numbers. As of July 2011, one million dolls had been made by thousands of mothers, grandmothers, great-grandmothers, students, and knitting clubs. Coincidentally or accidentally, the Izzy Doll project has turned into one of the biggest country-wide peace projects Canada has ever seen.

Authors Note: Often Boomer Caps are packaged with Izzy Dolls to distribute to children of all ages. Even our American friends; knitter's groups south of our border have taken up the call to make Izzy Dolls.

The only known photo of Mark giving a child a doll - he was always taking the pictures.

THE VOICES OF THE PEOPLE

"Therefore search and see if there is not some place where you may invest your humanity."

Albert Schweitzer

Knitting needles and crochet hooks in hand, the Izzy Doll makers have the same things in common. They are filled with compassion, recognize the suffering in the world, and are compelled to do something about it with what they have. Their contribution is more than dolls; it is their intent to make the world a better place. Through their actions, like many of the soldiers, they are making a difference. Here are just some of the quotes from correspondance from the knitters and soldiers, as well as others who have invested in humanity with a little doll called Izzy.

"When Lynne and I first walked into the HIV and aids orphanage run by the Franciscan Nuns at Bondo in East Africa with bags of Izzy African Comfort dolls for the kids, we came away in tears even though the dolls brought much joy to the wee tykes. Many were covered with end stage HIV ulcers, which were treated with the med sups we brought — pain killers (half an aspirin gives a suffering child a night's sleep), dressings and antibiotic ointments from Canada. When you enter a large room filled with baby cribs with two and three kids to a crib and you hear the moans of suffering children, one realizes how lucky we are to live here in the land of plenty. Children born with aids live from two to six years normally. So we are not saving the world, just easing suffering by the kindness of Canadians from sea to sea to sea. These wee tykes are buried with their dolls, which they hug in death as they did and do in life."

Billy Willbond, ICROSS Canada

"They were orphans since they were born; they never touch a toy or receive a gift from their parents or anybody. One nurse told me that some orphans were refusing to put down their toys even when they are eating, taking a shower or sleeping … thinking that it will be stolen… I can hear now birds singing because I was hearing only crying and fighting…Thank you Jesus for the good people that helped our people in Congo"

From Pastor Juntin Byakwli, (Congo)

"ORBIS is a non-profit organisation dedicated to saving sight. Since 1983 it has operated in over 60 missions worldwide. Dr. Brian Leonard, a Vitreoretinal Surgeon, is one of the many professionals who travels abroad and donates his expertise so others can see. ORBIS packs Izzy Dolls on their missions and Dr. Leonard has seen the effect the dolls have on the children. About the Canadian crafters he says, "There is a special place in heaven for all the knitters who make the Izzy Dolls for the children.""

"My dad was in WWII from '39 – '45 and I remember him talking about the conditions people were living in. In Holland he was shocked to see people were eating grass and flower bulbs. I thought of how much joy a little doll could bring to a child who had nothing. The dolls would be something that belonged to them, a friend to talk and play with…This is something we have the talent and expertise to do. It's our chance to do something special in the world."

Cass Dagg-Murphy, Tillsonburg, Ontario
Hickory Hills Izzy Doll Coordinator

"You hear about all the terrible things that happen in the world and where these things are happening, there are our dolls. I feel like I'm reaching out to people world-wide"

Margaret Englander, a knitter, Hickory Hills Izzy Group

"I couldn't get over the fact that these tough, battle weary soldiers put their own lives at risk to travel for 30 minutes just to deliver our dolls to the little children. It brought tears to my eyes and a lump to my throat. It made me proud to be a Canadian. May god bless them all and keep them safe."

Barbara Nanavati

"I am now in a retirement home. But I am glad to say I have knitted 30 dolls. I am 93 yrs old! And whatever my hands could do, it gave me great pleasure."

Gladys Roberts, Kanata, ON

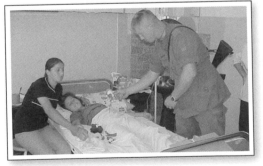

"It was at the Calgary Military Museum where I saw and read the story about The Izzy Doll … I was very moved by the story — amazed really… to find such kindness in a very dark time for kids … such a small little knitted doll could connect people in such a strong way."

Sandi Riemersma

"… our wee dollies have become a very important and cherished part of my life. I believe I have around 70-80 'black faced' dollies ready for delivery, sent along with much love, with more to come…"

Joan Sheep

"My Guide unit is diligently working on their dolls. They won't be the best but they will certainly be made with love. The parents are thrilled that we are doing this with the girls."

Susan Pulfer
Girl Guides Kitchener, Guelph and surrounding area

"I found your card in my mother's knitting basket. She was in her 83rd year and suffered from a heart condition. My mother, Sylvia, took great pleasure in making Izzy dolls. She knew the dolls would go to children who had very little. Sylvia hated the idea of children not having a toy. I want to thank-you for working on this project. The Izzy Doll Project gave my mother a lot of pleasure and a sense of purpose in her final years."

Sheila Merkley

"Good Evening William,

Just a short note to let you know there are two boxes of Izzy dolls well on their way to you from Truro N.S. We also have knitters on PEI and NB that says the Maritimes. 758 dolls make up the 2 boxes. Hopefully we will have as many next spring to send to you. Lots of love in the box and lots of good work go with the dolls. Blessings go to all who work for this cause."

From a letter to Billy Willbond from Doris

"We embraced the "Izzy doll" and gave them out with pride in all the bad places we were sent to serve. I hope you know that those little Izzy dolls also helped us preserve our personal humanity despite the destruction and misery we experienced."

Major General Ed Fitch

Darryl Preece

"I had an amazing experience working with the kids in Haiti. To see so many smiling faces and how much fun some of these kids where having even after all they have gone though. Going to one of their hospitals to work with some of these kids and family that were looking for help, just handing out a hand made doll brought so much joy to some of the struggling. This was a life changing moment for me."

Master Corporal Darryl Preece, Wing
Telecommunication & Information Service Squadron in Haiti, 2010

"Thank you for the Izzy African Comfort Dolls they bring great smiles of joy."

LCol Sandi Banerjee Canadian Peacekeeper in the Sudan

Ms. O'Connell,

Well, I finally made it to Sudan and was introduced to a Girl Guide troop by a female Canadian police officer working here with the UN. Your dolls were such a hit! These girls have nothing, not even uniforms and we managed to give all 300 guides two dolls each. We still have almost 2000 left but I am off to visit a couple of refugee camps in the coming weeks. If you only knew how happy these girls were with your dolls, you would get an indication of my appreciation for all the hard work you and your colleagues have done. Thank you again and I will be in touch.

Yours Aye,
George Forward (email to Shirley, 2011)

Cpl James Oakley and Cpl Kyle Scott were two Peacekeepers who were part of what they referred to as a "very special mission from our chain of command" during Op ATHENA, Roto 2 in Kabul Afghanistan.

Cpl James Oakley wrote:
"Our mission was to go into a local village and give out 'IZZY' dolls to children in the area. It was December 22, and even though the locals do not celebrate Christmas, we were in the spirit to deliver toys to children, especially when the people in that part of the world have to live with the kind of crushing poverty we saw every day."

The troop gave out the dolls and Cpl Oakley said: "Before I realized it, the box was empty and there were dozens of happy little faces milling around, enjoying their new treasures. As a soldier it can be tough to be away from family over Christmas, but the work of Carol Isfeld, and missions like the one I have tried to describe, help to make it worthwhile ... Touching the hearts and minds of people in war torn countries through these simple gestures is something we, as Canadians, do and should be proud of."

Cpl Kyle Scott wrote:
"We engineers had a never ending list of tasks to complete from route recces, conventional munitions disposal (CMD), counter IED - VBIED operations, minefield breaching, construction tasks, and base security/quick reaction tasks."

Pens were an item Cpl Scott said the children loved to get and he remembered their reactions. He went on to say, "Often there were not enough pens mailed from home, so I would raid the section commander's desks and steal all non-essential writing utensils. The look on a child's face after receiving something so insignificant to us was pure unconditional happiness; they would often break out into a dance or just yell. I often remember those faces and sounds, the simple joy you can bring to someone who has nothing. We take it for granted all too often back home."

Cpl Scott had heard about the Izzy Dolls and was excited to be a part of this special mission. "Those of us at 1CER had long heard the stories of MCpl Isfeld and his mother Carol's 'IZZY' dolls. I could not have been more proud to be a part of something so special. As soon as they saw the brightly coloured dolls, they went crazy! In such a bleak coloured landscape the dolls stood out like a rainbow in the dark sky ... I wondered if those small gestures of friendship would remain in the hearts and minds of the young Afghans."

IZZY'S LEGACY

Along life's path for all to see,
You have left your precious legacy.
All the things in life you learned,
The faith and love you took — you earned.

Your gift was giving because you cared,
Now others feel the love you shared.
And so my son, around the world,
Your flag of love has been unfurled.

Your dolls are carried far afield,
The love they carry is your shield.
With marching feet, hands hold them high,
And the dolls hear each and every cry.

A loving soldier stoops to say,
"Here's love for you, no tears today."
And many helpers heard the call,
So loving hands make "Izzy's Doll."

Our care is stitched in every part,
So every doll has got a heart.
Though mine don't have a little face,
The thought of yours is in that space.

Your eyes and smile a child can do,
Each one will know it came from you.
I feel you still so many ways,
Your memory fills my nights and days.

In life you made so many friends,
Seeds of love, that never end.
Dolls are sprouting far and wide;
I can feel your hug and smile with pride.

Carol Isfeld, Aug 14th 2000

165

CHAPTER 9

WAR AND PEACE

Phyllis Wheaton, Mother, Grandmother, Singer, Songwriter

"we had some instructors from the British Army. one day while practicing bayonet fighting - jabbing dummy men. the instructor came up to me and said, "Put more into it! Just imagine these dummies are German and you hate Germans don't you?" I said, "No. I don't hate anybody." He turned around to the men and said "Blimey. some of these Canadians are funny blokes." one day later he came over and said "I guess none of us really hates anybody."

This quote is from Personal Memoirs of the
First World War:Poor Bloody Murder edited by Gordon Reid.
It is on an interpretive board at the Stones of Signal Hill in Calgary

LEST WE FORGET

THE MASK OF ANTI-WAR

To keep the peace in our family my mother always said, "kids, just get along." with the lift of one eyebrow she sent an unspoken expectation that we were to do something to get along; take turns, be nice, be patient, share. with eight kids in the family peace was not easy and didn't just happen. We had to work at it.

Phyllis Wheaton

My interest in the lives of soldiers and their families did not go unnoticed. Some of my friends and acquaintances thought I was writing songs, and now a book, about war. They stated they were anti-war with what I took to be an unfair tone that seemed to imply I was trying to justify war. Somehow the word anti-war was synonymous with anti-soldier even though that was about as accurate as blaming a doctor for the cancers of the world. The fact was that I was trying to pay tribute to those I perceived as the 'forgotten' ones — the families who had survived the death of a soldier, their son or daughter killed while in the service of our country. These were the families no one talked about.

I had worn my own anti-war mask in the past without giving it much thought. However it began to shift after I had archived the letters of WWI soldier David Argo, and it came right off after meeting the Isfelds. I was now questioning whether my use of the word 'anti-war' was actually indifference or maybe apathy under the guise of the great protest label. I thought of Mark's phrase "in the mood for peace" and wondered whether my actions were a testament to the fact that I had the right attitude, or whether the mask just diverted attention from my actions — or my inaction — for peace. I can make a guess as to what Mark might say to me, "So you're going to use the word 'anti-war' to make yourself feel better? But what are you doing with what you have to contribute to peace?"

I have learned that wishing for peace is different from actually being a contributor to it. It is easy to become paralyzed or feel inadequate or cynical about the woes of the world, or to expect that the needed change will come from others. But being in the mood for peace, I believe, is being in a state of awareness of what needs to be done and then acting on it. Carol Isfeld showed the compassion we need, Brian illustrated how to right the wrongs, and Billy and Lynne Willbond are examples of what can be accomplished when people persevere through difficult roadblocks.

Mark chose to de-mine. He put his life at risk along with his 1CER brothers who, as Mark said, "think about the lives they save but not the one they risk." After his death, his parents, despite their grief and pain, continued to bring smiles to children's faces and hope to their hearts with the Izzy Dolls. It was their way of doing something, contributing their drop toward a growing sea of compassion.

I thought the world had come a long way with the concept and implementation of Peacekeeping. When Brian and Carol told me about the landmine ban I was surprised because that meant "peace for all" wasn't a fantasy — it could happen and was happening. In fact, Brian was certain that our world could be landmine free and that "it can happen in our lifetime."

Banning landmines and clearing suspect land was an exciting prospect and a welcome mindset that focused on action. The creating and stockpiling of instruments of war is a mindset also. It implies that we expect war. Eliminating landmines worldwide means we expect peace, or at least we expect conflict to be resolved differently than in the past. It also means that all parties agree that eventually conflicts end and life after war will resume. Therefore their vote to ban landmines meant that post-conflict landmine tragedies were no longer acceptable.

Brian told it like it was. He said that in the past, one of the jobs of the combat engineer was to plant landmines. However, as a Peacekeeper his son's mission was to remove them. Now, with the Ottawa Treaty our soldiers will never have to plant landmines. At least in theory.

But some countries are still holding out and have not signed the treaty. If the goal of a landmine-free world is to be achieved, every country has to make a sincere commitment - if they too are in the mood for peace.

THE NEW SOLDIER?

"In an age of intelligent, educated, thoughtful soldiers in more ambiguous moral situations the burden of what we do and see can be all the greater. I try to be positive about it; once we have been witnesses, we have a responsibility to take action and tell of what we have seen in a way that will tend to improve the situation."

Major General Ed Fitch

As I listened to the parents of our soldiers tell their stories, there appeared to be a lot of similarities in their children's characters and moral fibre. I wondered if there wasn't another phenomenon — whether a new type of soldier was evolving. I wasn't alone. Journalist Andy Holota suggested Mark Isfeld could have been the epitome of this new breed. Andy said the new soldier is not only tough, skilled, and courageous, he or she is compassionate. Not only is the new soldier educated and well-trained, he or she is knowledgeable and thoughtful.

Major General Ed Fitch, (Retired), who was Mark's commander after CFSME, explained that a 'new' soldier could exist, "particularly since the advent of armies of conscripts, but even more so since 1990." He identified the word 'thoughtful' as a descriptor of such a soldier. "I have known many soldiers who have been good at their profession and, indeed, very brave in battle, but their experiences do not weigh on them because they do not think about them nor the implications of what they see."

Since the 1990s, Ed explained, there was "relative ease with which families could send 'stuff' - transport capacity, speed of delivery, free postage from Canada to a theatre of operations." He also said, "I sense that soldiers have always given what they could, especially to children, but latterly we have more to give and more opportunity to be in contact with the affected population." Timing and technology are factors in the 'new soldier phenomenon' but it is also the result of the values of the society they grow up in.

In 1996, CBC's *The Journal* aired a video report by Nancy Durham called *The Engineer* which highlighted the Peacekeeper's work. In it Ed described his life's work as a calling, not just a job. He said he cringed at the behaviour of the officers of the former Yugoslavia who instructed their young soldiers to destroy and kill based on ethnic and religious lines, perpetuating hate and prejudice. He said he questioned what kind of lessons they were teaching; what kind of human being they were shaping.

A soldier reflects the society they are raised in, so Canada with its values of equality, tolerence and freedom fosters an environment where a 'new soldier' could very well emerge. Legacy projects like the Izzy Doll, Boomers Legacy, and the Landmine Ban are all extensions of a society that believes in their responsibility in the global village. Collaboration between a 'thoughtful' soldier and his loved ones at home who send aid packages is also powerful philanthropy. I think Arilius would be proud of both soldiers and civilians, for taking the direction he prophesied back in 1967 — to do our part as global citizens and members of the world community.

SUPPORT OUR TROOPS

"We can't afford to not afford to look after our soldiers. We can't afford to not afford to lift those mines"

Leigh Isfeld about the cost of deployment

Carol's message to take care of our troops and our veterans was not only about her compassion for others. It was something she had learned when her uncle was denied a military pension in the late 1950s.

Uncle Bjarnie Hannibal Paulson was a Corporal in the Royal Canadian Air Force and one of approximately 600 military personnel who walked into an arena where no one else wanted to go. He assisted in the 1958 cleanup at the Chalk River Nuclear Facility in Ontario after a fuel rupture and fire in the reactor building.

Hannibal had adhered to the strict code of secrecy for twenty years until his health deteriorated to the point it jeopardized his ability to make a living. Doctors blamed his exposure at Chalk River for the rare cancerous tumours and 'holes' in his skin, which resulted in dozens of operations.

The incredible stress on Hannibal and his family could have been relieved by a veteran's pension. However, he was denied one when the Atomic Energy of Canada Limited (AECL) stated there was no record of him ever having been at the Chalk River Nuclear Facility. Discouraged and depressed, he wondered how many others had been forsaken by the RCAF and the AECL.

Eventually, after involving lawyers, Hannibal did receive the pension he rightfully deserved but the respect owed to Hannibal and the soldiers who had been deployed to Chalk River came much later.

Kareen Jackson, Hannibal's eldest daughter, told of an interesting mail delivery in 2009, twelve years after her father's death. It was an official commendation, signed by the Minister of Foreign Affairs, Peter Mackay, for Hannibal Paulson's work in the Chalk River cleanup in 1958.

There are many more stories of other soldiers and their families who claimed to have had to fight for just compensation. One military wife told me of her attempt to get financial support when her husband was ill and died from job-related causes during the Cold War. Because of the top-secret nature of his role, compensation was impossible to obtain, leaving her to raise her daughters without financial help.

I've met the last of the Atomic veterans — a group of forty soldiers who marched alongside American soldiers into the Nevada desert on a military exercise during the cold war. They performed war games less than 1,000 yards from an atomic blast and then repeated it five more times. An award winning film by De La Ruelle Productions called *Time Bombs – 40 Canadian Soldiers, 6 Nuclear Bombs, 1 Secret* tells their story. The few men who are still alive and the wives of those deceased are still trying to get the government to notice them, to talk, and to settle.

The families of our soldiers have long known what Ombudsman Yves Côté brought to the forefront in his 2006 report titled *Heroism Exposed.* Although he was referring to the exposure to the toxic smoke from the burning oil fields in Kuwait in 1991 and to radiation from depleted uranium shells, his message was clear. As stated in a news conference and in a CBC news story dated November 1, 2006: "The legitimate health concerns of soldiers were not given the weight they deserved. If we send our [soldiers] abroad healthy and they return sick, they need to know that Canada, their country, will take care of them."

Regardless of what decade or the party in power, in too many cases it appears to be the government position to wait for veterans to complain or sue for compensation. It was Carol Isfeld's message that whether our soldiers are deployed abroad or sent to natural or man-made disasters at home, we must take care of them and support them like family — as a mother would. She would have echoed Mr. Côté and would have probably sent him an Izzy Doll for his brave convictions to stand up for our children.

Authors Note: I remember hearing stories about my grandfather when I was a little girl. He had returned from WWI with shellshock and was treated like an outcast. People in his community did not understand his condition which today would be called PTSD.

The account of Mrs. Willbond feeding the WWII soldiers who were sleeping under the Ottawa bridge reminded me of how little was known about PTSD decades later.

In recent years the psychological and scientific research around PTSD and the changing attitudes in the military have led to a collective will to do something about the treatment of PTSD. Family education and counselling are just a few of the options now open to soldiers and their loved ones coping with this life-altering condition.

As a point of interest, an organization called National Service Dogs has proven that trained canines can be effective with children with autism and special needs. As of 2011 they have developed a program called Skilled-Companion Dog for Veterans, to help soldiers and veterans with PTSD transition back into their lives.

HEROES ARE MADE NOT BORN

THE SOLDIER POET'S MOM

God and the Soldier we all adore
Was written by a fine poet who had been to war
For whatever reason, thoughts that are now long gone
To this very day he remains, an ANON
The danger passed and all things made right
Forget about God. And of the soldier make light
Missing limbs, poor pension, no home and no bed
They called the soldier a bum. That's what they said
That soldier named Sarge he was never a bum
Though he drinks cheap wine, said the poet's kind Mom
He's a thing called shellshock and sad memories it seems
That poor man he suffers from some very bad dreams
Monica Willbond fed the soldiers and her nine kids
With a pot full of Irish stew. It's a kindness she did
She made us all kneel and say a round of the beads
And ask God to provide for that poor soldier's needs
Many years later when Monica Willbond had died
at the back of the church some old soldiers cried
There sat the Sarge and his friends, who had been to AA
Now getting handicapped pensions, from Canada's D.V.A.
For the funeral, this poet, he came home on leave
And he spoke to the Sarge who had come there to grieve
Your Mom is a saint Billy – She's now an angel up there
An angel down here, she fed the poor when no one would care!

Billy and Lynne Willbond and the ICROSS Canada story makes me smile, and all the colourful characters involved in their quest to ease world suffering makes me joyful. Each generation influenced the next and their family torch continues to be passed down and willingly accepted.

Grandmother to son, officer to soldier, knitter to student, and veteran to volunteer are all relationships that testify to the idea that heroes are made, not born. ICROSS Canada volunteers encourage each other, lead by example, and continue to persevere even through difficult times. They are proof that there is a hero inside all of us.

The story of ICROSS Canada, from the knitters and crocheters, the bikers, the vets, to the volunteers at Compassionate Resource Warehouse, is simply happy. Billy wouldn't let it be otherwise. His fearless momentum has cracked through red tape, corruption, and roadblocks; he is an example of a soldier who never gave up.

Despite all this success, Billy is not complacent. He knows that, volunteers eventually have to retire from their position, so new volunteers are always required.

Then there are the logistics and costs of shipping donations of hospital equipment across this vast country to the Compassionate Resource Warehouse on Vancouver Island. Recycling surplus thousands of miles away is not easy. But Billy does not dwell on the negative. He has learned that people continue to arrive, like angels, and the good work continues.

The flame of compassion burns brightly in the Willbond family and the torch of goodwill is passed down to the next generation.

Families relocated from the Kibera Slums to their new home in the Shamba.

HEALING PROPERTIES OF CREATIVITY

"Painting is poetry that is seen rather than felt, and poetry is painting that is felt rather than seen."

Leonardo da Vinci

In everyone there is a soldier and a poet.

We all have an artistry inside ourselves that can be roused by an urgency to communicate something important. This inner creativity is as natural as laughter and as cleansing as tears. Art helps us reframe difficult emotions, present abstract concepts, offer up unorthodox ideas and explain what seems to be the unexplainable.

The link between the spiritual and the creative has long been recognized. Artistry is the expression of our unique presence and who we are as individual spirits living on a material plane. It is also through the arts that the remnants of our existence are documented and recorded for generations to follow.

While researching for this book I wasn't surprised to find music, painting, photography, filmmaking, and writing turning up repeatedly as people found relief and expression through their creativity.

It was poetry that showed up most often in these stories. Parents, siblings, soldiers, and veterans used this medium to help reframe their emotions. Sometimes they used rhyme, metaphor, or lilt to make their feelings concrete and palatable so others could understand. Sometimes they wrote purely to vent what was deep inside and had to come out. It is all an example of what I've labeled the Isfeld Formula: do something (write a poem), with what you have (feelings and memories), and a positive outcome — from understanding to healing, to creating a change — will result.

The craft of storytelling is one of the oldest forms of art, both for entertaining and for the preservation of history. There are many examples of expert storytellers in this book, from the NFB film crew with *The Price of Duty*, and W5's *Heart of Darkness* to independent filmmakers and journalists in other mediums. Music, the pen, new technologies as well as print and radio all contributed toward the narrative that inspired Canadians with the Izzy Doll story and the Isfeld messages.

It was the combination of the spiritual and the creative that Brian recognized in the open-minded Padre Monpas. The Padre's signature optimistic viewpoint was that "God is good, She understands and She is forgiving." He also knew the challenges related to trying to forge ahead into unknown territory with an idea.

Legacy projects are a creative mind-set, spirited by family members who want to do something to immortalize their child and create something that enables that child's memory to live on. But like anything worthwhile and meaningful it takes a lot of focus and comes with a caution. Padre Monpas explained that the new world that a family creates around a legacy project can sometimes orbit the deceased, leaving the living, breathing family in the shadows. He said many families have contributed wonderful legacy projects that have had a positive impact on the needy and on the world, but it can be a delicate balancing act.

Many artists have related that their best ideas have emanated from their greatest pain. Projects like the Izzy Dolls, Boomer Caps and Boomer's Legacy are examples of creations that have emerged from the deep pain of loss. Each project has gained momentum and morphed into a huge collage of people and deeds. If we could frame each project as a work of art then hang them on a wall and step back, we would see portraits of ourselves and how Canadians are being led by these families to play a vital role in the world.

Children adore their Izzy Comfort Dolls

An infant wearing a Boomer Cap with and Izzy Doll

Students wear Boomer Caps in the school in the Shamba that ICROSS Canada built

THE GOOD-BYE MELODY

The week before Brian passed, I was in an interview at a school. My cell phone rang and I was embarrassed that I had not turned it off before our meeting began. I reached for it and saw it was Brian Isfeld's telephone number on the tiny screen. The staff member understood that I needed to take this call, and she left the room. I thought it was Pat calling to notify me that Brian had died, but to my surprise it was Brian. His voice was weak and hoarse, "Don't talk. Just listen. Sing me *Good-bye*, four times."

Just the day before, I was commiserating that Brian had told his friends not to send any 'junk', as he called it. No flowers, which is the traditional gift sent by well wishers to make us feel better because we did something. Now here he was calling from his deathbed, literally, to ask me to sing the song *Good-bye*. In his own way he was inviting me to give him something — if I was up to the challenge.

Good-bye was one of the songs Brian had requested David O'Toole and I perform at Carol's memorial. It was written by Paul McCartney and made a hit by Mary Hopkins in the sixties. Other than the title, I questioned his choice of song for his wife's memorial. But he seemed sure of himself. Now with his departure looming, the lyrics were ever so poignant, as if meant for him and Carol. He knew I would get the correlation.

The last verse of the song talks about a lonely lover who has gone on, almost implying it could be to a heavenly place. She sings a plaintive song calling to him; he accepts her invitation and goes to her.

I choked back the tears trying to rise to his challenge to sing this not once but four times, and for a cry-baby like me it was a huge challenge. Somehow I got through it once.

With a weak and gravelly voice he said, "Sing it again."

I sang it again conscious that the staff member could hear me belting out a song while she waited outside the door. It must have seemed strange.

"You owe me two more," said Brian, ending the phone call abruptly as he passed the phone to his sister.

His statement that I owed him two more bugged me. I didn't want to owe him and he was going to a place where I wouldn't be able to give him the last two songs, so with the help of the guys in the band we scrambled to get a copy of *Good-bye* recorded and in the mail.

Brian died the following week and I received a thank you email from Pat, "We took his Good-bye CD to him in hospital, and on the day he died it played many times over."

They had played it more than twice, including at Brian's funeral, and Pat said I didn't owe him any more.

***

Like Carol, Brian also donated his corneas so others could see. As they did in death so they did in life — the Isfelds had helped me to see, to realize the complexities of war and peace and my part in it.

Since beginning the writing of this book I have felt their presence urging me to keep going. The most recent affirmation was on Peacekeepers' Day August 2011. Leigh and Judy and their son Mark drove from Edmonton to Calgary to deliver additional photos for the book. I suggested they come on the Sunday and take in the Peacekeepers' ceremony, which they did. It just so happened that the Seventh Book of Remembrance was on a tour from Ottawa with its own entourage and set up at TMM for public viewing.

The museum had apparently been quite busy. During the half hour or so that we were there, a *Calgary Herald* photographer arrived to take a photo of the Seventh Book. It was interesting that Leigh, and his family were asked to pose in front of the book of the dead, Judy pointing out Mark's name on the calf vellum page. I watched and grinned. This was the book that was missing when Carol Isfeld was the Silver Cross Mom. Now here it was for her son and his family to view. It was also interesting that the book had been here for two days but the photographer showed up coincidently during the small window of time when the Isfelds' son, daughter-in-law, and grandson were visiting.

The next day a large photo of Leigh and his family was in the *Calgary Herald* with the story about the Seventh Book of Remembrance and its visit to Calgary. It wasn't a coincidence.

***

If by chance the colourful flying train in Brian's last dream is still flying through the heavens — and if by chance it stops in to pick up the mailbag, then I'd like there to be something in it for them.

Dear Mark, Carol, and Brian,

Here are your stories clothes-pinned together for all the knitters and crafters and volunteers to read and to understand the beginnings of the Izzy Doll. I'm certain your stories will encourage even more people to do something with what they have and to make the world a better place, just as you did.

Thank you for all the omens and affirmations along the way that gave me the confidence to forge ahead. I have learned so much about the great people that make up our country — ordinary people accomplishing the extraordinary, just like each of you, one kind gesture at a time.

Now it's all been said. Right?
Rest in Peace my friends.

Phyllis

INTRODUCTION TO THE ORIGINAL "IZZY DOLL" ASSEMBLY

The Izzy Doll, Copyright Carol Isfeld. Not to be used for financial gain

Written by Carol Isfeld

The doll is made up of a series of "Slinky-like" coils crocheted separately, then knitted together solidly to form a body, arms, and legs. A head is crocheted, stuffed with synthetic "Cotton Batting," attached to the main body, then a hat is sewn on; either a UN blue beret for the "Boy doll," or pigtails, braided hair etc., and a bonnet or floppy hat for the "Girl doll." Synthetic materials (Carol liked to use variegated colors) are used to prevent shrinking if doll gets wet. The overall size is five to 6 inches in height, and about 4 inches in width, including the arms.

A CARD with the picture of Mcpl Mark Isfeld, and a small inscription is attached (to the doll) (made from business cards printed on the computer).

"IZZY DOLL", Made for you with love, in memory of MARK ISFELD,

killed near Kakma, Croatia 21 Jun 1994, removing landmines

serving with 1 Combat engineer Regiment, Canadian Engineers.

(Your name and address here, if desired.)

I will write down below the general method I use, attempting to explain it the best way I can.

178

BODY

All measurements are approximate. The body will be about 1 3/4 inch in width, and will be about

2 ½ inches in height. I use ordinary synthetic white wool as the starting point, or "base", on which to crochet the coloured coils. Shown here **Fig01** is the last coil with the white "base" and the blue portion left to enable sewing it together. (Leave approx. 12 in) The first coil has only the white "base" wool extended to facilitate binding together. See **Fig02**

Use hook # 4.5 - 5, and 4 ply wool. Chain 50 - 60. In each Ch., 3 D.C, (double crochet) until last Ch.

It will curl as you go, so straighten and flatten curls, and coil to form body.

Curls should be about 1.5 -2 inches across. When coiled you should have 10 - 12 rings. Align Ch.'s, sew up and down to secure and compress body, not too tightly, and secure wool at the top. ALL pieces have wool left long to enable sewing together, and ALL ends are crochetedinto work to maintain neatness. After sewing the body, **Fig03** you will note that the end **Fig04** that you start on forms a slight depression, and this is where I attach the head.

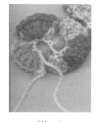

Fig 1

Fig 2

Fig 3

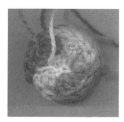

Fig 4

LEGS - ALWAYS LEAVE WOOL TO SEW WITH AT EACH END OF WORK

As with the body, but with a different color 4 ply wool, using 4.5 - 5 hook, Ch. 30 - 40. In each Ch.,3H.D.C -3 timcs to curl (as body) to last Ch. Sew to secure, as done with the body. Work should be 10 coils, approx. 3/4 inch across. **Fig05** Compress and sew as for the body, leaving lots of wool strands at each end to facilitate sewing together to form the doll. At the point where the "foot" is I put in a little bit of different color wool. For sewing together, I separate strands of 4ply wool and use it. Attach one leg at a time to the body securely, sewing up and down through the body, tying tightly at the top. When finished both legs (or arms, depending on size) it looks like this **Fig06**

Fig 5

Fig 6

ARMS

For the arms use a 3 hook and 2ply wool, Ch 20 - 30----1SC 3 times in each Ch. Till the last stitch, then sew up and down to compress and form the arm. Arms measure about 1 1/4 to 1 ½ inch in length and ½ to 3/4 inch in width after compressed and sewn tight. **Fig06a** Attach each to the body side, and sew up and through the body, securing at the top. **Fig07** You now have a partly completed doll looking like this **Fig08**

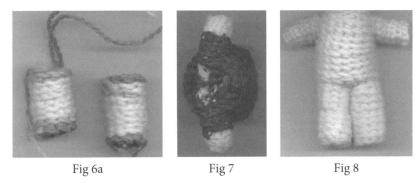

| Fig 6a | Fig 7 | Fig 8 |

HEAD

Basically you make a sphere in which to pack compressed synthetic "cotton batting". Using 2 ply flesh colored wool and #3 hook, Ch 5 and join to first Ch to make a circle 2SC in each Ch.Repeat to keep flat until work measures about 1 inch (3 or 4 rounds) Continue 1 Sc in each Sc until work measures 2 inches across, keeping it flat, like a little rug. Start to decrease (2 together) every 4th or 5th Ch slowly; As work curls down form a circle, decrease until you have a small hole, stuff with synthetic batting then sew closed leaving wool ends to attach to body. Head should be about 2 inches in diameter. **Fig09** , **Fig09a** Attach the stuffed head to the body top, sewing in and out through the top, hiding the stitches and securing tightly. It now looks like this

For the girl dolls, using bright yellow 4 ply wool, make braids by assembling from 7 inch lengths of wool (12 in all) and make three strands using four lengths in each. **Fig11** Gather at the center, leaving lengths of wool to attach to head, braid down each side, add little pieces to make bangs or curls, and attach to the side of the head forming the pigtail, or braids. Your finished braids will look like this **Fig11a**, **Fig11b**

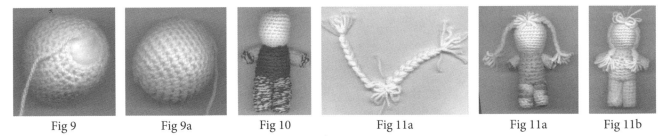

| Fig 9 | Fig 9a | Fig 10 | Fig 11a | Fig 11a | Fig 11b |

HATS Fig12d

Peascekeeper's Hat

A basic half sphere is formed sort of like a 'tam o'shanter." **Fig12** Using 2 ply med. blue wool and #3 hook chain 5 to join to first Sc to make a circle as you did for the head, increasing once each row until it measures about 2 ½ inches. It will start to curl down. About 12 rounds from the start and 1 inch deep, continue Sc in

each Sc until work is about 1 ½ in deep, and you have decreased enough to fit the head. Now change and add black wool for the band, leaving ample to sew the hat to the head. **Fig12a** Using gold wool, embroider a small circle to simulate the UN hat badge as per this image. **Fig12b** Now attach to head, Pull the right side down and secure to the side of the head. **Fig12c**

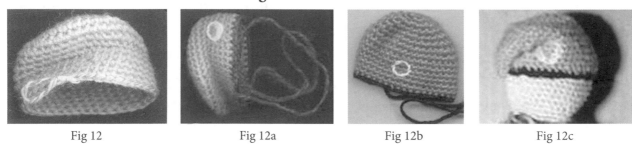

Fig 12   Fig 12a   Fig 12b   Fig 12c

Girl's hat - Can be made as per image here, **Fig13** or get any small hat pattern from a craft book, or make up your own! Use gaily coloured wool, and attach with experimentation - you can make a bonnet, or a floppy hat or anything!

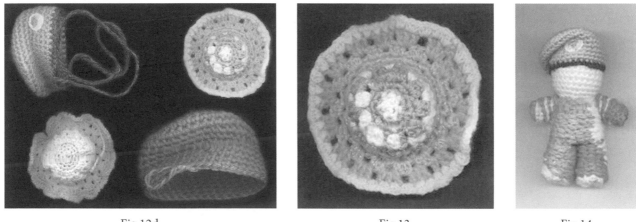

Fig 12d   Fig 13   Fig 14

WEB SITES OF INTEREST

Cpl Mark Isfeld memorial site and Izzy Doll pattern	www.izzydoll.ca or www.izzydoll.com
ICROSS CANADA (Izzy Comfort Doll pattern here)	www.icross-canada.com or www.icross.ca
Boomers Legacy (Boomer Cap Pattern here)	www.boomerslegacy.ca
Operational Stress Injury Social Support **- contact for the program of H.O.P.E.**	www.osiss.ca
International War Veterans Poetry Archives	http://iwvpa.net
Double Tap Awards	http://iwvpa.net/awards/index-dta.php
Billy Willbond poetry page	http://iwvpa.net/willbondwha/
The CAV motorcycle web site	www.thecav.ca/
Veterans Affairs Canada news/information	www.veterans.gc.ca
NFB Price of Duty online	www.nfb.ca/film/price_of_duty/
National Service Dogs	www.nsd.on.ca
Hannibal's full story	www.ccnr.org/paulson_legacy.html
Canadian Coalition for Nuclear Responsibility	www.ccnr.org
Canadian Atomic Veterans web site	http://canadianatomicveterans.com
Nichola Goddard 'Light Up the World'	www.nicholagoddard.com
Daniel Gunther website	http://pages.infinit.net/danieldo/daniel/
National Defence and the Canadian Forces	http://www.forces.gc.ca
Icelandic Connection Magazine	www.icecanmag.com/

ANTI-LANDMINE WEB SITES

There are dozens of organizations worldwide who are committed to removing unexploded ordnance left by war. Here are a few:

The Canadian Landmine Foundation	**http://canadianlandmine.org/**
Canine demine project:	**http://canadianlandmine.org/projects**
Mine Actions Canada	**www.minesactioncanada.org/**
The HALO Trust U.K. and U.S.A.	**www.halotrust.org**

HALO Trust is the world's oldest and largest humanitarian landmine clearance organization.

International Campaign to Ban Landmines (ICBL)　　**www.icbl.org**

This campaign started in 1992 when six groups formed a partnership to ban anti-personnel landmines: Human Rights Watch, Medico International, Handicap International, Physicians for Human Rights, Vietnam Veterans of America Foundation, and Mines Advisory Group. They were instrumental in organizing the Ottawa Treaty and won the Nobel Peace Prize for their efforts.

Center for International Stabilization and Recovery　　**http://maic.jmu.edu/**

Mine Detection Rats　　**www.apopo.org**

APOPO is a Dutch acronym that stands for Anti-Persoonsmijnen Ontmijnende ProductOntwikkeling or translated, Anti-Personnel Landmines Detection Product Development. Founded by Bart Weetens, a Belgian, this non-profit organization trains African giant pouched rats named HeroRats, which are highly effective and cost efficient, to detect land mines.

ACRONYMS AND TERMS

Sapper or Combat Engineer:	A soldier whose duties range from bridge-building, laying or clearing minefields, demolitions and road and airfield construction
Cpl :	Corporal
Sgt :	Sergeant
PT :	physical fitness training
CFSME :	Canadian Forces School of Military Engineering
RCAF :	Royal Canadian Air Force
PPCLI :	Princess Patricia's Canadian Light Infantry
CFSME :	Canadian Forces School of Military Engineering
NCO :	Non Commissioned Officer
Section :	8 - 10 soldiers
Troop :	approx 35 soldiers
Squadron :	approx 80–110 soldiers
Regiment :	approx 300–600 soldiers
Brigade / Division :	approx 3000–15,000 soldiers
1CER :	1 Combat Engineer Regiment
CDS :	Chief of the Defence Staff
MND :	Minister of National Defence
CIDA :	Canadian International Development Agency
CAVUNP:	Canadian Association Of Veterans In United Nations Peacekeeping
UN :	United Nations
UNPROFOR :	United Nations Protection Force
NORAD :	The North American Aerospace Defence Command
NATO :	North Atlantic Treaty Organization
SAR :	Search And Rescue
CBC :	Canadian Broadcasting Corporation
NFB :	National Film Board
CANLOGBAT	Canadian Forces Logistics Battalion
PAFFO	Public Affairs Office, national Defence
PTSD :	Post Traumatic Stress Disorder
OSISS :	Operational Stress Injury Social support
OSI :	Operational Stress Injury

IED :	Improvised Explosive Device
H.O.P.E. :	Helping Others by Providing Empathy, Program of peer support
PROM-1 :	a type of anti-personnel mine
CMD :	Conventional Munitions Disposal
MAD Site :	Location for Munitions Awaiting Disposal
BIPS :	Blow In Place
Ordnance :	military reference to weapons, ammunition, combat vehicles, and equipment
UXONS :	are Unexploded Ordnance ie: bombs, bullets, shells, grenades, landmines, naval mines, or any other explosive weapons that did not explode when they were employed. UXONs that are not detonated pose a risk until they can be located and appropriately disabled.
VBIED :	Vehicle-Borne IED
APC :	Armoured Personnel Carrier
M.S.M. C.D. :	Meritorious Service Medal, Civil Division
ICROSS Canada :	International Community for the Relief of Starvation and Suffering, Canada
CAV :	Canadian Army Veteran
PTP :	Physicians Travel Packs
OES :	Order of the Eastern Star
CRW :	Compassionate Resource Warehouse
HPIC :	Heath Partners International Canada
W.O.W. :	Women for Orphans & Widows
ORBIS :	Greek for 'of the eye' and is an international NGO dedicated to saving sight worldwide
AA :	Alcoholics Anonymous
AATF :	Assistance to Afghanistan Trust Fund
ICBL :	International Campaign to Ban Landmines
MAC :	Mine Action Canada
CLMF :	Canadian Landmine Foundation
MAPA :	Mine Action Programme for Afghanistan
MDD :	Mine Detection Dogs
CIDC :	Canadian International De-mining Corps
LSN :	Landmine Survivors Network changed its name to Survivor's Network
AECL :	Atomic Energy of Canada Limited
CAVA :	Canadian Atomic Veterans Association
TMM :	The Military Museums formerly Museum of the Regiments

PHOTO CREDITS

Most of the photos in Mark's chapter were taken by him. All photos in this book are credited to the Isfeld family archive except for the following contributors:

Pg. 2	Stones of Signal Hill - Fred Bagley
Pg. 3	Mae and David Argo - The Military Museums
Pg. 3	Phyllis at Ellon Memorial - Ted Bartlett, Scotland
Pg. 41	1CER Brotherhood
Pg. 44	Memorial Cross - www.veterans.gc.ca
Pg. 59, 132, 133, 134, 136, 159	Captain Sheppard - Shirley O'Connell
Pg. 158	Derrick Gaudet photo - Steve Sadler
Pg. 61, 153	LSN
Pg. 71	Carol's memorial photo - Teanna Hodgins
Pg. 74	Brenda Livingston
Pg. 93	Jim Davis
Pg. 97	Ben and Margie Walsh (with Jeffrey)
Pg. 107	Padre Monpas and Isfeld family - Sgt Rebecca Bell DND
Pg. 112, 175	Boomer title page, baby with Boomer Cap - Maureen Eykelenboom
Pg. 116	W. Brett Wilson
Pg. 123	CRW Dell Marie Wergeland
Pg. 118, 119, 120, 125, 127, 129, 173, 175, 186, 187	Billy Willbond / ICROSS Canada
Pg. 130, 131	Mike Comeau
Pg. 131	Mollie Colson
Pg. 138	Didsbury Hospital Auxiliary - Sharon Barefoot
Pg. 138	St. Martin's Anglican Knitters - Vic Ramsbottom
Pg. 145, 154	Children on the artillery and Princess of Wales - HALO Trust
Pg. 149	Kong Chim - Jennifer Lonergan PhD
Pg. 163	Master Corporal Darryl Preece
Pg. 170	Hannibal Paulson - Kareen Jackson
Pg. 44, 73, 91, 97, 101,102, 177	Mikey and Carol, Group photo - P. Wheaton
Pg. 81, 166	Blue Beret and 'Lest We Forget' - Diana Slater
Pg. 70, 158, 166	Dolls - David Bull
Pg. 166	Phyllis and guitar - Lawrence Chrismas
Pg. 155	Canine - Scott Fairweather, CLMF